THE PROCESS OF LAWFULLY OPERATING A HOSPITALITY BUSINESS IN INDIA

DR ANSHUMALI PANDEY

Contents

Preface

The process of LAWFULLY operating a Hospitality business in India:

This Book consists of almost all the Laws, rules and regulations which are mandatory to operate any hospitality business like Hotels, Bars, Restaurants, etc in India. When I say 'almost' I mean that with the ever changing and updating rules and regulations, you can't be 100% sure if you have done everything right. The rates of the long list of Licenses needed for hospitality business in India are reasonable and nominal. But the things which I cannot mention in an academic book is that, to obtain those Licenses you might not pay only the License fee as mentioned in the govt charts but much more than that. Thus the cost of hospitality business compressed under regulations and expenditure is not all that rosy as it seems to an unsuspecting customer.

However, this book will give you all that are needed to keep yourself away from problems which may engulf you if caught unaware by the long arms of the Law and the gleeful agencies responsible for implementing those Laws. I would say "it's better safe than sorry". Follow all the rules and try not to be tempted to take any shortcuts. After reading this book you will have better understanding of the Hospitality Unit operations and will give you an opportunity to think one more time before taking a plunge in the industry as an entrepreneur. Finally, and more importantly for me, after reading this book you will have more respect for the people associated with Hospitality Industry.

Dr Anshumali Pandey, PhD, Author.

Prologue

In today's fast pace world, the hospitality manager's need to be multi-talented & multitasked individuals. Besides, their domain knowledge of Hotel operations like Food & Beverage Production & Service, Room Division Operation's, Marketing, Revenue Management; they are required to assume specialized roles such as employee counselor, facility engineer or computer system analyst. In today's highly competitive & diverse business environment, the skill level required for success today in this field is greater than it was in the past.

Hospitality Management has always been a very challenging & precision perfection profession. This is exhibited in their multi-faced roles like in a casino operation, 5-star hotel, Outdoor catering, In-flight catering & Industrial Catering operations.

Day after day, in hundreds of situations, the action of operational mangers of Hotel's will influence the likelihood of the business or the manager becoming the subject of Litigation.

Almost all the activities in Hotel operations & Tourism Industry is covered by legislation. Most of the legislation pertains to the start of Hotel operations & Tourism. but some of the aspects are complicated and need expert's advice time to time, so as to resolve the legal requirements.

ONE

INTRODUCTION TO HOSPITALITY LAWS OF INDIA

INTRODUCTION:

In today's fast pace world, the hospitality manager's need to be multi-talented & multitasked individuals. Besides, their domain knowledge of Hotel operations like Food & Beverage Production & Service, Room Division Operation's, Marketing, Revenue Management; they are required to assume specialized roles such as employee counselor, facility engineer or computer system analyst. In today's highly competitive & diverse business environment, the skill level required for success today in this field is greater than it was in the past.

Hospitality Management has always been a very challenging & precision perfection profession. This is exhibited in their multi-faced roles like in a casino operation, 5-star hotel, Outdoor catering, In-flight catering & Industrial Catering operations.

Day after day, in hundreds of situations, the action of operational mangers of Hotel's will influence the likelihood of the business or the manager becoming the subject of Litigation.

Almost all the activities in Hotel operations & Tourism Industry is covered by legislation. Most of the legislation pertains to the start of Hotel operations & Tourism. but some of the aspects are complicated and need expert's advice time to time, so as to resolve the legal requirements.

LAW (DEFINITION):

Law can be defined as a universally accepted body of rules that aims at creating a social system that encourages people to interact voluntarily in a civilized manner; as and when there will be an infringement or a violation of these regulations, the judicial system steps in to enforce order by the imposition of penalties. The study of law is a challenging aspect as it varies from state to state in India. Example: - The legal drinking age in Goa state is 18 years and 25 years in Punjab state.

Historical Origins of Law:

Common Law and Civil Law are the two major systems of law in place across western world & Sovereign Indian. Common law is the body of law that descended from Great Britain and is used in India and most countries in the British Commonwealth. Whereas, The Civil Laws have descended from the Roman Empire and is used extensively across the five continents. Both these types of laws work in close proximity to each other. One of the major contributors for the Common Law was Sir William Blackstone. Between 1765 A.D and 1769 A.D, he wrote four volumes titled the *Commentaries.*

The Future Hospitality Manager and the Legal Environment:

Hospitality managers demonstrate the multi-faced roles of securing raw materials, producing a product or service and selling it – all under the same roof. Besides, all these the Hospitality Managers has direct contact with the guest, the ultimate end user of product & service supplied by the industry.

Additionally, Hospitality Managers are called upon frequently to take decisions that will impact the legal standing of the employer. This means that the Hospitality Managers have to work in close tandem with Law Specialist like the Attorneys.

The Hotel Industry, an important constituent of Hospitality Industry is operational 24/7 X

365. This simply means, that day after day, in hundreds of situations, the actions of these managers will influence the likelihood of the hotel business, probably becoming the subject of Litigation. According to the experts in Hospitality law makers & formulators, the law is constantly changing and evolving; learning the law today might make this same as absolute in few years.

The Hospitality Manager to begin with should:

- Know the Historical origins of the specific laws.
- Recognise that the law will change & evolve, primarily based on the changes of the society / state / sovereign country.

- Understand the manner in which to effectively use a philosophy of preventive management.
- To manage the existing legal environment and minimize the chances of litigation

INTRODUCTION TO HOSPITALITY INDUSTRY:

The major thrust of Hotel and Tourism Laws are to govern & regulate the activities of the professionals, guests & other related entities. The laws provide an assurance of their professional competency &stability. In this process the professionals of Hotel & Tourism Industry acquire legal status by way of legislations. This legislation in turn clearly defines the professional's roles in both the industry. It invariably means to cover tourism & hotel industry categories and activities like –

- The conditions imposed on each category
- The protection given
- Legal provisions of the acquirer's controls
- Illegal acts
- Loss of license

In order to keep the above categories & activities intact, the following legislations need to be enacted –

1) Laws that will regulate the professional status of Travel & Tourism Industry

2) Laws that govern the professionalism of tourist guides

3) Laws that will govern the professional status of

a. Hotels, Resorts,

b. Food & Beverage establishments like – Bar, Pubs, Restaurants, Fine Dining, Snack-bars, Fast-food outlets

c. MICE Companies (Meeting, Incentive, Conference & Exhibition companies)

d. Recreation & Entertainment facilities like Amusement Parks, theme-based parks

e. Other Hospitality & Service Industries

4) Laws governing the Foundation, organization & Management of

a. Associations&

b. Federations of Tourism

c. Hotels & Resorts

d. Food & Beverage Establishments

Hotels – Definition:

An establishment whose primary business is providing lodging facilities for the general public and which furnishes one or more of the following services.

- Housekeeping service
- Food and beverage service
- Bell and door attendant service
- Laundry and dry cleaning
- Concierge
- Use of furniture and fixtures

HOTEL CORE AREAS – (Revenue Earning Departments):

Front Office Department- It is Responsible for Welcoming & registering the guest, allotting rooms & Helping guest checkouts. It is headed by Front Office Manager

Housekeeping Department- It is responsible for cleanliness & upkeep of front of the house areas as well as the back of house areas. This department is headed by Executive Housekeeper.

Food & Beverage Service Department- It constitutes the Restaurants, Bars, Coffee Shop, banquets & Room Service. This department is headed by Food & Beverage Manager.

Food Production Department- It constitutes the Kitchen & Bakery. This department is headed by Executive Chef.

HOTEL SUPPORT AREAS:

Maintenance Department- This department is responsible for all kinds of maintenance, repair and engineering work on equipment‘s, machines, fixtures, and fittings.

Human Resource Department- Recruitments, Orientation, training, employee welfare, compensation, labor laws & safety norms of the hotel are under preview of Human Resource Department. This department is headed by Human Resource Manager.

Sales & Marketing Department- The function of this department is 5-fold – Sales, personal relations, and advertising, getting MICE. This department is headed by Sales & Marketing Manager.

Financial Control Department- Inventory control procedures are the responsibility of this department. This department is headed by Financial

Controller.

Security Department- This department is responsible for safeguarding the assets, guests and employees of the Hotel. This department is headed by Chief Security Officer.

Purchase Department- The procurement of all departmental inventories is the responsibility of purchase department. This department is headed by Purchase Manager.

LEGAL PERSPECTIVE:

Legal requirements in Hotel operations covers the following areas: -

- **Premises** – It covers Electricity, Fire precautions, Food and Drugs, Food Hygiene, Food Premises, Sarai Act, Shops and establishment, Public Health & Lifts & Escalators
- **The Food** – Food, Food safety, Food Hygiene and Regulations, Food Premises, Food labeling, Trade descriptions, Weights & Measures, Food, Preservation and Adulteration Act
- **The Drinks** – Licensing Act, Excise act, Children & Young Persons Act, Exercise Act, Food labeling, Weight and Measures, Alcoholic Liquor, Employment of women Act
- **The Music**–Copyright, Design and patents, Local Government, Licensing, Public Health, Control of Pollution.
- **Personnel Health & Safety** – Health and safety, Personal protection to equipment‘s, Provision and care of work equipment, Work place regulation, shops &establishment, Explosives
- **Personnel: Employment** – Conciliation and arbitration, Disabled persons, Statutory sick pay for employees, Employer‘s liability, Employment Act, Employment protection, sex discrimination, social security, time off to public duties, Trade unions, Minimum wages, Industrial disputes, Bonus, Holiday and Retirement benefits, Gratuity Etc., Payment of wages, Excise Act, Sarai Act: Boarding and Lodging Establishment Act
- **The Business** – Indian Companies Act 1956, Partnership Act 1932,Insolvency, Data protection, Marketing, Sales of Goods, Contract Act, Price indications, Consumer Protection, Theft, Rent contract act, Foreign Exchange Regulations, Environment & pollution control, Registration of Foreigner‘s, Essential commodities Act, Carriage of Goods Act, Insurance Act, Prevention of Food adulteration Act.

Power of Local Authorities:

The local authorities by enforcing Acts & bye-laws make provisions in the building for escape routes or emergency exit in case of accidental fire (man-made calamities) or other natural calamities.

Laws Relating to Hotel Premises:

To start Hotel operations, an entrepreneur or promoter needs to construct new building, permission from local authorities & laws need to be sought. Alterations to existing building for operational aspect will also need permission from local authorities with a focus on effects on neighborhood.

- **Electricity**: -The regulations will cover electrical systems, equipment's and Appliances. Only qualified personnel should be appointed for the use of these equipment's.

- **Fire Precautions**: - A Fire certificate becomes compulsory under the Fire Act for Hotels & other Hospitality Institution's.

- **Sanitary Conveniences**: -The local municipal authority requires the Hotelier's, Public houses, entertainment establishment and other service related organization's to comply with minimum sanitary conveniences.

- **Water**: -The local authorities which are responsible to supply water fix charges per 1000 cubic meters of water, subject to right of authority with minimum payment.

- **Advertisement**: -Only illuminated Display advertisement in the business premises, related to the specific business needs permission from the local authority.

Laws related to Planning & Designing:

The principal aspects with respect to Hotel & catering industry are as follows:

-

- **Access**: - Access is required from nearby streets and roads, both for guests arriving in cabs & other forms of transport. Separate entrance for guests & staff in Hotel premises, enhances the in flow and out flow of people.

- **Parking**: - Parking and turning space for guests of Hotels or restaurant's is collaborated with its Room Capacity of Hotel and or seating capacity of Food & beverage outlets.

- **Surroundings**: - The hotel or Restaurants site should blend well with its surrounding landscape.

- **Visibility**: - The Hotel or catering Facility should be in clear visibility from Main road. The sign board should be strategically located, so that maximum visibility is seen while accessing the property.

- **Guest Entrance**: - the Hotel's or catering establishment Guest entrance is to be well designed and have wide access to the main road.

- **Line of Glass Door at Main Entrance**: -A line of Glass door at Main entrance of Hotels or restaurants gives a clear visibility to the lobby of hotel or the reception area of the restaurant.

International Hotel Regulations for Hotels and Guests:

The contractual agreement between the guest and Hotel begins the moment the reservation request is accepted by the Hotel.

The contract is subject to: -

- The law of the nation wherein the hotel is located.
- The regulations enforced in the hotel premises.
- International Hotel regulations.
    - The contract entitles the guest to occupy the accommodation he has reserved & make full use till the check-out date.
    - To use and avail the benefits of the services and product [food &beverages] offered by the Hotel. It also includes the use of sitting area of lobby or terrace lounge Etc.

The guest recognizes the following: -

- The reservation of the Rooms is entitled to him / her and the names mentioned in the Reservation.

- The Guests accepts the reservation with simultaneously accepting the agreed room tariff and the meal plan (if any).
- Also, on confirmation of Reservation, the offer price of product (Food & Beverage) is deemed final and will be charged as per usage of the guest.
- The Guests cannot cook food in their allocated Rooms.
- If the guest brings in alcoholic or non-alcoholic beverages which are available in the Hotel; the Hotel has the right to charge Extra for the same.
- The Guest is responsible for all damages done by him, his associates, servants or his guests. Hotel has the right to charge for all collateral damage done by them.
- The Hotel has the right to give preference to guests who reserve Rooms with Meal plans or package plans (Guests who are willing to avail more of the Hotel facilities besides the Room accommodation).
- The Guests are not permitted to bring pets to the hotel without the prior consent of the Hotel Management.
- The Hotel Management has the right to cessation or diminution of resident guests due to undue noise, nuisance, disturbance to other guests, and violation of ethics.

International Laws for Food Safety, Quality & Security:

There have been several international organizations & agreements playing a role in enhancing food safety, quality &security etc.

Codex Alimentarius Commission –

FAO & WHO jointly established the food standard programmed& adopted the status of the CAC. The body responsible for completing the standards, code of practice, guideline &recommendations that constitute the Codex Alimentarius. This is an international food code. It creates standards that protect consumer, ensuring fair practices in the sale of food &trade, food control administration & traders.

Codex India – It is the national codex contact point (NCCP). Itacts as a link between the codex secretariat &Indian member body, coordinate all codex activity in India, receive all text & working documents, and promote codex activities throughout India.

WTO – World Trade organizations begin in 1995. The benefits of it are –

- The system helps to promote peace.
- Rules make life easier for all.

- More choice of product & quality
- Trade raises income
- Trade stimulates economic growth
- The basic principal makes life more efficient.
- They cover good services & spread the principals of liberalization.

ISO – International Organization for standardization is a worldwide federation for national standardish is a non-government organization established in 1947. The mission of ISO is to promote the development of standardization &related activities in the world with a view to facilitate the international exchange of goods &services, & to develop cooperation with technological &economic activity. ISO 9000 is concern with quality management.ISO 14000 is concern with environmental management.

FAO – Food &Agricultural organization - It is founded in 1945with a rise level of nutrition & standard of leaving. Now it is a leading agency of to collect, analyzed, interpret the information related to nutrition agriculture, forestry, fisheries & rural development.

WHO – World Health Organization – It is established on 7th April 1948.To set the objectives of highest positive level of health? The main functions are as follows:

- Articulating ethical &evidence-based policy.
- Managing information by assessing trends & comparing performances related to development.
- Changes through technical & policy support
- Negotiating & sustaining national & global partnership.
- Monitoring the validity on proper purchase & standard.
- Development new technology, tools & guide lines in health care management.

LEGAL PROCEDURE:

Legal Procedure: The Journey of a Case through the Courts.

If a Hospitality organization wants to allow the case to go for trail,

1. Should you allow the Case go to Trial?

Factors to considered are – Time requirements, Cost factors, Reputation/ publicity

2. To be successful in a lawsuit the plaintiff must prove the following:

a. The defendant violates the law

b. The plaintiff suffered injury or loss

c. The cause of the injury or loss was the defendant's violation of the law or a tort

3. Steps to a Lawsuit

a. Commencing the lawsuit b. Trial

4. Complaint

a. Completed by:

I. Completed by your lawyer.

ii. Will complete with assistance from the clerk of courts (If not having a lawyer)

b. Statement of jurisdiction: Information provide must provide the court/ defendant enough information to answer the following:

5. Summons

a. Document ordering the defendant to appear and defend against the allegations /complaint

b. Contains the information of Complaint, Time limit for response &Consequences of not responding

6. Service of Process

Delivery of summons

I. Laws vary by state

ii. Refusing to accept a summons does not mean you were not served

iii. Failing to respond to a summons will result in a default judgment

7. Response to the Complaint

a. Preliminary motions: Written requests for relief /dismiss the lawsuit /change of venue

b. Answer: c. Motions directed to the answer

d. Reply: e. Summary Judgment

8. Pre-trial Procedures

a. Discovery: The processes in which both sides obtain evidence know to the other side. Information is obtaining by:

I. Questioning the other side ii. Inspection of physical evidence.

iii. Review of documents held by other side or witness

iv. Mental or Physical examination.

9. The Trial

a. Type of trials: b. Steps to a trial c. Selection of the jury

d. Opening statements: e. Case-in-chief

f. Plaintiff's case in rebuttal g. Summation

h. Judge's charge to the jury I. Jury deliberation

j. Rules for deciding the case l. Judgment m. Appeal

10. Appellate court: Hears appeals.

a. First attorneys submit either written brief or written arguments.

b. The attorneys can be scheduled for oral argument if the court decides to hear the case.

c. Appellate rulings:

11. Alternative Dispute Resolutions

a. **Arbitration**: A third party listens to the evidence in an informal hearing and rules. In most case the decision cannot be appealed.

b. **Mediation:** A mediator facilitates the discussion and tries to help both parties reach a mutually acceptable solution. Mediator does not have the authority to impose a settlement.

c. **Summary jury trials**: Primarily use in federal courts. Attorneys present arguments to an informal jury. There are no witnesses called and the verdict is nonbinding.

KEY ISSUES:

The key Issues in Hotel operations by a Manager includes the Legal Requirement's in Hotel Premises, The Food &Beverage, Background soft Music, Personal Health &Safety, Employment& Business Sustainability.

The Law & Ethics:

In Hotel operations, The Managers many a times face a situation wherein, their activity may be legal, but still the wrong things done. It is this distinction that all future Hospitality Manager's need to identify & implement who are seeker's to manage their own legal environment & that of other employees working in the establishment.

In Hospitality industry, Ethical behavior refers to the behavior that is considered —right

—or —right things to do —. The operational managers & staff's need to consistently Choose ethical behavior over behavior that is not ethical in order to avoid any legal difficulty. In the case of any litigation, the jury members of the courts will have to make determinations of whether a manager's action were intentionally ethical or unethical. How these jury members and judges of the court decide these questions will determine their views on a manager's liability for an action or inaction.

Example 1: - A Situation in Banqueting operations of a Town Hotel

Assume that you are the Manger responsible for a large wedding reception of a hotel. You require a large amount of wine and champagne, as it is the wedding of the MP's daughter. You have ordered for 5000 Nos of bottles of the premium Dom Perignon Champagne. The guaranteed guests were 8000 in numbers from all over the country and abroad. The other guests of the prime list included 3000 in numbers. The party started at 07:00 p.m., but at 12:55 a.m., the stock of Dom Perignon was exhausted. You took a decision to open additional 1000 no's of Taittinger Champagne. The party went off very well. The MP personally thanked the General Manager for the smooth manner of operations for this very large numbers. Now, as a Banquet Manager, should you charge all 6000 no's bottles at the premium brand – Dom Perignon rate, or give a consolidated discount on complete 7000 no's bottle billing or do actual billings for the 5000 no's + 1000 no's separately, with an apology of not intimating during the course of function?

In certain cases, it is difficult to determine what will constitute an ethical behavior. In such scenario, the following seven guidelines proves useful while evaluating a possible Course of action:

- Is it fair?
- Am I honest?
- Would I be concerned, if it happened to me?
- Would I be in the position to publicize my action?
- Is it legal?
- Does it hurt anyone?
- What if everyone does it?

Example 2: -An Ethical Situation in Hotel operation.

Assuming that you are the Food & Beverage Manger of a Large Hotel. You are on a hectic plan for the upcoming New Year's Eve Plan. You have a high requirement for Wine and Champagne in particular. For this you have asked for a competitive rate from your regular supplier's. Based on the already booked parties across all your 7 Banquet Halls, 2 Party Lawn Banquet's & 3 outstation Buffet orders; you have ordered for wines and champagne worth Rs. 20 Lakhs from your long-term supplier and lowest bidder M/s. Primus Hospitality Services. A few days later, an International supplier of champagne sends you a case of expensive wines to your home and with a note that they are looking forward to meet you at the earliest, so as to have a futuristic long-term business association. What will you do with the case of champagne?

The Ethical Analysis: Your first and foremost reaction would be to drink at least one bottle to have a feel of the champagne bottle. But, on a professional outlook you need to ask yourself 7 basic questions (which is the core of Ethical Analysis).

The 7 basic questions are: -

1. **Is it legal?** - It may be very much ok or acceptable from a personal level viewpoint. But does the state or national law permit such actions? This clause or action or reaction needs to be checked.
2. **Does it hurt anyone?** - This more on the conscious level of the employee. If it really does not hurt anyone, then we can move to the 3rdquestion.
3. **Is it fair?** - Before answering this specific question we need to see and analyses who the stakeholders are in this particular situation.
4. **Am I being Honest?** This specific question gives the employees of the hospitality industry a second check for question no 2 & 3.
5. **Would I care if it happened to me?** - For this specific question, every employee whether at supervisory level or managerial level, needs to place themselves in the shoes of the proprietor and then relook at this question. The solution outcome will be the actual.
6. **Would I publicize my action?** - This is more of an imaginary situation. if your action in the hotel as a supervisor or manager is made public on TV or newspaper, will it be acceptable to you.
7. **What if everyone did it?** - This being the last question every employee needs to ask for himself. If your action is duplicated in some other forms across all departments by their members, will it be acceptable to hotel operations.

<u>THE LEGAL REQUIREMENT PRIOR TO DOING HOTEL BUSINESS:</u>

Key Consideration's for Starting a Hotel Business:

In India, the Central and the state government s view business and individual's as two distinct entities.

The key considerations for starting the Hotel business are enlisted as:-

- **Incorporating the Hotel Business:** The ease and cost of incorporating the hotel operation's
- **Control:** The power of control of the individual that he / she would exercise on the Hotel business entity.
- **Finance:** The Capital investment required & all possibilities of securing Institutional finance.

- **Taxation:** The Goods & Service Tax (GST) structure applicable to the Hotel Rooms, Food & Beverage products and their related services.
- **Liabilities:** The liabilities of Hotel operation's and the individual owner.
- **Transfer of Ownership:** The ease of exiting the Hotel business if required.

Formation of a Hotel Company:

There are three stages towards the formation of a Hotel Company: -

- Promotion Stage
- Incorporation Stage
- Commencement of Business Stage

Promotion Stage: -

The Hotel business entrepreneur or promoters after conceiving the idea of Hotel operations would

- Determine the quantum of the capital required

- Explore the different sources of finance to start the operation's

- The entrepreneur or promoter does the incorporation of Hotel business as either one of the following: -

§ A Private Limited Company

§ A Public Limited Company

§ A Partnership Firm

Incorporation Stage: -

The law will be applicable based on the very nature of the company incorporated.

- If the Hotel operations are incorporated as a public limited company or private limited company, then it is under the companies act, 1956.

- Similarly, if the Hotel operations is incorporated as a partnership firm, the partnership deed will need to be made. This will be followed by registration under the Indian partnership Act,1932.

- Lastly, if the hotel operations area limited liability partnership firm, it will be required to form under the Limited Liability Partnership Act, 2008.

Commencement of Business: -

- A private limited company can start business with the incorporation of public limited company through a Commencement of Business (COB) Certificate from the Registrar of Companies.

- A partnership Hotel firm or a limited liability Partnership Hotel organization can commence the Hotel operations after receiving the certificate of Registration.

THE LEGAL REQUIREMENT AT THE TIME OF DOING HOTEL BUSINESS:

For the successful completion of Hospitality business, it is more of a binding commitment for Corporate Hotel & Hospitality Managers to fulfil obligations towards guests, employees and other like suppliers & contractors on broad terms. The above laws get amended, on time to time basis, this means, that the Laws will keep changing or updating from time-to-time. The Laws in India keep changing by Amendments of Courts or through the acts of parliament.

Every Hotel, Food & Beverage establishments needs to provide the following information to the Registrar's Office:

1. Name of the employer and the Manager
2. Area of the premises
3. Value of the premises
4. Existing water and light connections in the establishment
5. Required necessities like water connections, lighting connections, Ventilations, Environmental norms or Laws & Safety Laws.
6. Number of employees on
    a. Permanent Role
    b. Contractual basis
    c. Daily wages
7. Medical Benefits & other fringe benefits provided to the employees
8. Contribution to Employer's Provident Fund (EPF), Group Medical Insurance, Group Life – Insurance, Units linked Insurance Plan (ULIP)Etc.
9. Registering the employees with Central Government & state government schemes
10. Name and the Registered address of the company
11. Category of the Food & Beverage Service such as Kiosk, Coffee shop, cafeteria, Restaurant or any other.
12. Category of Hotel from1 star to 7 star or from Heritage Hotels to Heritage Grand.

SUMMARY:

Hotel law plays a vital role at multiple stages of operations. One should understand the correlation between Future Managers and Legal Environment. By studying this lesson, one can understand Indian

Hospitality Industry, legal requirement prior to doing Hotel Business &lastly, legal requirement at the time of doing Hotel Business.

GLOSSARY:

- LAW (Definition):- Law can be defined as a universally accepted body of rules that aims at creating a social system that encourages people to interact voluntarily in a civilized manner; as and when there will be an infringement or a violation of these regulations, the judicial system steps in to enforce order by the imposition of penalties.
- Common Law and Civil Law are the two major systems of law in place across western world & Sovereign Indian.
- Hospitality – Definition - (Oxford Dictionary) Hospitality is defined as: Reception and entertainment of guest, visitors or strangers with liberality and goodwill.
- Hotel core areas - revenue earning department are front office department, housekeeping department, food & beverage service department & food & beverage production department
- Legal requirements in Hotel operations covers Premises, The Food, The Drinks, The Music, Personnel Health &Safety, Personnel: Employment & The Business
- Laws Relating to Premises are Electricity, Fire Precautions, Sanitary Conveniences, Water & Advertisement.
- Laws related to Planning & Designing are Access, Parking, Surroundings, Visibility, Guest Entrance & Line of Glass Door at Main Entrance
- The 7 basic questions of Ethical Analysis are: - Is it legal? Does it hurt anyone? , Is it fair? , Am I being Honest? , Would I care if it happened to me? , Would I publicize my action? & What if everyone did it?
- Key Consideration's for Starting a Hotel Business are Incorporating the Hotel Business, Control, Finance, Taxation, Liabilities & Transfer of Ownership
- Three stages of the formation of a Hotel Company are Promotion Stage, Incorporation Stage & Commencement of Business Stage
- The legal requirement at the time of doing Hotel Business are Name of the employer and the Manager , Area of the premises , Value of the premises , Existing water and light connections in the establishment , Required necessities like water connections, lighting connections, Ventilations, Environmental norms or Laws & Safety Laws , Number of employees on Rolls , Medical Benefits & other fringe benefits provided to

the employees , Contribution to Employer's Provident Fund (EPF), Group Medical Insurance, Group Life – Insurance, Units linked Insurance Plan (ULIP) Etc. , Registering the employees with Central Government & state government schemes , Name and the Registered address of the company & Category of the Food & Beverage Service such as Kiosk, Coffee shop, cafeteria, Restaurant or Category of Hotel.

TWO

LAWS OF HOTEL OPERATIONS IN INDIA

INTRODUCTION:

The term 'Company' is derived from the Latin word *Companis*, which means to break bread together. It was also referred as an association of persons who took their meals together. An improvement upon the partnership model during the Mauryan times (timeline – 322 B.C to 185 B.C) in the form of *Sreni* was seen. In the western world during medieval times, the guild of merchants had the closest resemblance to a Sreni and modern-day companies.

In India, the Companies act, 1850 was modeled on the basis of England's Joint Stock Companies Act of 1844. Later, the Companies Act, 1913 in India was again modeled on the basis of England's Companies Act of 1908. After Independence, with the introduction of this bill in parliament & approval of President of India, The Companies Act, 1956 came into force with effect from 1st April, 1956. Besides, this Act, The Indian Partnership Act, 1932 and the limited Liability Act ,2008 laid the groundwork towards formation of today's Partnership Firms and Limited Liability Partnership (LLP) firms.

DOING HOTEL BUSINESS IN INDIA:

In India, after Independence, the business environment has been very restrictive with a sole aim of protecting Indian companies from foreign competitors. The Monopolies and Restrictive Trade Practices Act, 1969 (MRTP) coupled with Foreign Exchange Regulation Act, 1973 (FERA) discouraged entry of foreign Institutional Investors (FII) and Foreign companies to do business in India. The ease of doing business slowly, but steadily improved post 1993 with liberalization of Indian Economy. This change brought in many Multinational Hotel companies post 1993 in India.

Introduction to Hotel Business:

The business structure that emerged with the implementation of the laws in form of –

- Sole Proprietor
- Partnership Firm
- Limited Liability Partnership (LLP) firms
- Private Limited Company
- Public Limited Company

In addition to the above, the following types of business options are also available for foreign investors or foreign companies desirous of doing business in India:

- Liaison Office
- Representative Office
- Project Office
- Branch Office
- Wholly-owned Subsidiary Company
- Joint Venture (JV) Company

In India, the conceptualization of a limited liability company, which is to be limited by guarantee, after its files two primary documents – The Memorandum of Association and Articles of Association.

Memorandum of Association:

The Memorandum of Association is a document that sets the constitution of the company and defines the relationship of the company with outside world. It states; -

- The Name of the Company
- The type of the company
- The Objective and scope of the company
- Authorized Share Capital of the company
- Name of the subscribers (original shareholder's) of the company

Articles of Association:

The Articles of Association lays down the rules and regulations for the internal management of the company for achieving the objectives stated in the Memorandum of Association. These rules cover the following: -

Issuing of shares

- The different voting rights attached to the classes of shares.
- The different dividend rights attached to the classes of shares
- Restriction on transfer of shares
- The rules for conducting Board Meetings
- The rules for conducting Shareholders Meetings

Representative Office:

These are Offices either established across India as branch office or attached as office of other place of business. The Hotel's in India have to update the Representative office i.e. Foreigner's Regional Registration Office & Local Intelligence Unit (ILU) after the Registration of Foreigners. For tourist from Pakistan &China, the ILU gets each registration details within few minutes if processed online or has to be given by Hotelier within 12 to 24 hours. The Foreign Exchange Management Act, 1999 is enacted by Reserve Bank of India (RBI) in order to provide temporary Money Exchanger License to Hotels.

Definition - Representative Office

Further, As per the Foreign Exchange Management Act, 1999 and Foreign Exchange Management Regulations, 2000, (Establishment in India of Branch or Office or Other Place of Business)

"a Liaison Office / Representative Office means a place of business to act as a channel of communication between the Principal place of business or Head Office by whatever name called and entities in India but which does not undertake any commercial / trading / industrial activity , directly or indirectly , and maintains itself out of inward remittances received from abroad through normal banking channel ."

Liaison Officer:

With respect to FEMA notification No. 12 /2000 RB dated 3rd May 2000, Schedule II, a liaison officer can engage in the following activities: -

- Represent the parent company or group of companies in India.
- Promote the export / import from / to India

- Facilitate both or either of technical/ financial collaborations between parent or group companies with other companies in India
- Act as channel for communication between parent company or group of companies with other Indian companies.

Foreign Exchange Management Act, 1999:

Foreign Exchange Regulation Act (FERA) was incorporated in 1973 with the objective of

- Regulating foreign business in India
- Maintaining exchange Rate Stability
- Conserving & cushioning foreign exchange reserves

The changing economic scenario led to the passing of Foreign Exchange Management Act (FEMA) in 1999. This Act is more economic friendly, as it had

- Consolidated and Amended laws relating to foreign exchange
- The objective of facilitating external trade and payments

Capital Account Transactions:

These transactions alter the assets or liabilities, including contingent liabilities, outside India of an Indian Citizen or NRI. The transactions are referred to in section 6 (3) of FEMA.

Current Account Transactions:

These payments arise due to the connection with

- Foreign Trade
- Other current business activities and services
- Short term banking
- Credit facility in the business operations
- Remittance of living expenses of parents, spouse and children residing abroad
- Expense in connection with foreign travel, education
- Medical care of parents, spouse and children
- Payment due as interest on loans
- Net income from investments

Foreigner's Regional Registration Office: (FRRO).

Under the Foreigner's Act 1946 and Registration of Foreigner's Act, 1939; hotels need to furnish required details of all foreigner's to the

- Foreigner's Regional Registration Office (FRRO)
- Bureau of Immigration

For countries like Pakistan & China there is a mandatory upper time limit of maximum 12-24 Hours, due to sensitivity of National security. Hotel maintains a 'C' Form registration, besides the regular Guest Registration Card (GRC) for all foreigner's checking in Indian Hotel's.

Local Intelligence Unit (ILU):

The Local Intelligence Unit(ILU) is a specialized wing attached to police station. This department or section deals with all registration of foreigners who are staying in Hotel's within their premises. C Form again is the basis of documentation process between the Hotels and the Local Intelligence Unit (ILU)

Regulatory Issues:

Regulatory issues that affect the Hotel business environment are classified into the following: -

Taxation – Direct Taxes: -

- Goods & Service Tax (GST)
- Corporate Tax
- Dividend Distribution tax (DDT) Minimum Alternative Tax (MAT)
- Withholding Tax
- Wealth Tax
- Short Term Capital Gains (STCG) Tax
- Long Term Capital Gains (LTCG) Tax

Taxation – Indirect Taxes: -

- Service Tax
- Value Added tax
- Excise Duty
- Transfer pricing

TAXATION – DIRECT TAXES:

Goods & Service Tax (GST): The taxation under Goods & Service Tax (GST) is based on the range of Hotel tariff per night. The details of different slab rates are described in the following table: -

GST Rates for Hotels on Room Tariff, (March 2022 Data):

- **Tariff per Night : GST Rate**
- < INR 1,000 : No Tax
- INR 1,500 -2,499 : 12%
- INR 2,500 -7,500 : 18%
- > INR 7,500 : 28%

The Goods & Service Tax (GST) has replaced the Luxury Tax & surcharge on the Room Tariffs.

The following are the key rates applicable to GST on food services*:

- 5% GST on food services provided by restaurants (both air-conditioned and non a/c).
- 5% GST on restaurant services including room service and takeaway provided by restaurants located within a hotel featuring room tariff less than Rs. 7,500.
- 5% GST on any food/drink (non-alcoholic) served at cafeteria/canteen/ mess operating on contract basis in office, industrial unit, school, college, hostel, etc.
- 5% GST on meals/food services provided by Indian Railways/IRCTC or their licensees both onboard trains and on platforms.
- 18% GST on restaurant services including room service and takeaway provided by restaurants located within a hotel featuring room tariff over Rs. 7,500.
- 18% GST on food services including delivery of food provided by a restaurant/food joint located within premises of a club, guest house, etc.
- 18% GST applicable to all outdoor catering services provided.

*The list is indicative and rates are subject to periodic change.

Corporate Tax: - It is the tax payable by the Hotel Company on its income acquired over the just concluded financial Year. For the purpose of taxation, Hotel companies are categorized as either domestic or foreign companies, A public or private limited company or Management Control based company from the Indian sub-continent.

Dividend Distribution Tax: - Dividend Distribution Tax (DDT) is levied on domestic hotel companies as a charge on the dividends declared, distributed, or paid by companies to their shareholders.

Minimum Alternative Tax: - This specific tax was introduced in the year 1997-98 under section 115 JA of the Income Tax Act, 1961. The Government made Minimum Alternative Tax (MAT) payable by Hotel companies, if their taxable income is less than a certain percentage of the booked profits. Then, in this situation, by default the booked profits will be considered for taxable income.

Withholding Tax: - It is the tax that is deducted at the source from income.

Wealth Tax: - The Wealth Tax Act, 1957 stipulates that wealth tax is to be paid by any person or organization where the threshold limit of the net wealth is greater than Rs. 30,00,000. This tax is calculated at the rate of 1 percent of the amount exceeding the threshold limit.

Short Term and Long-term Capital gain Tax: This is incorporated when profit is made by the sale of capital assets. Example: - Sale of immovable property, Investment in shares, Mutual Funds or jeweler. Short term Capital Gain (STCG) Tax is levied when assets is sold within 12 months from the date of acquisition.

Long term Capital Gain (LTCG): Tax is levied when Equity shares, Mutual Funds, Debentures are sold after 12 months from the date of acquisition.

TAXATION – INDIRECT TAXES:

Service Tax: - It is paid by the service provider and is levied at 12.33 percent (Inclusive of educational chess and surcharge)

Value Added Tax: - After April 2005, Value Added Tax (VAT) has replaced the sales Tax. VAT is a multi-stage system of taxation on goods. As taxation happens in multi- stages of value chain, the end customer bears the brunt of this taxation.

Excise Duty: - It is charged on the manufacture of Goods and is payable by the Manufacturer.

Transfer Pricing: - Then laws relating to Transfer pricing was introduced in 2001 through 92A to 92F of the Income Tax Act, 1961. The purpose of the law was to ensure that the dealings are between two group companies or an Associated Enterprises (AE) located across borders followed by Arm‘s Length (ALP).

Business Contracts:

- Introduction to Contract

- Indian Contract Act, 1872
- Essentials of a valid Contract
- Types of Contract
- Performance of Contracts
- Steps to Follow When Drawing Up Contracts
- Hospitality Contracts
- Preventive Legal Management & Contract
- Negotiable Instrument Act, 1881

Introduction to Contract:

In Hospitality or Hotel Industry, Litigation arises because the plaintiff believes in one of the following to be true: -

- The defendant acted on something, for which he or she was not required to do it.
- The defendant didn't / ignored on something, for which he or she was required to do it.

In the above mentioned both the circumstances, the Operational Managers can land up in a confused situation, wherein it becomes difficult to understand what exactly the guests of the Hotel require in a complex situation. The peculiarity of the situations might extend to even these Operational Managers interaction with vendors and suppliers with whom he / she regularly interacts in operational process.

Contracts and Laws surrounding the External entities [Like Guests, Vendors, Suppliers, Tour Operators, Travel Agents, Online Travel Agents, Event Managers, Architectures, Building Contractors Etc] have to be established. This will lead both the parties to a mutual agreement that could be more clearly understood in terms of Agreement or Promises.

Indian Contract Act, 1872:

The purpose of the Indian Contract Act, 1872 was to introduce certainty to a transaction. It also voices the principles that make an agreement into a legally enforceable contract. The Act is divided into 11 sections dealing with various aspects of contracts. Section 7 (sale of Goods) was repealed when propagated, and Section 11 dealing with partnerships has been substituted in 1932 by the Partnership Act.

Essentials of a valid Contract:

In hotel operations, a valid contract is created when a hotel confirms a guest reservation against a deposit. The contract is validated, when the guest arrives at the airport and is received by the hotel representative. This is followed by Guest registration. The contract gets completed on allocation of Rooms to the guests. The essentials of a contract are: -

- Offer and acceptance.
- Intention to create a legal relationship.
- Lawful consideration.
- Capacity of the parties.
- Free consent.
- Legality of the object.
- Certainty.
- Possibility of performance.

Types of Contract:

During the hotel operations, there are times when contractual obligations are created even though there is no formal agreement such as quasi contracts. The different types of contract seen in hotels are –

- **Bilateral Contract:** -It is an agreement in which the participant parties make promises to one another.

- **Unilateral Contract:** -It is a contract wherein only one of the participant party makes a promise to pay upon the completion of a specified action or task.

- **Express Contract:** -The express contract is either in writing or orally expressed between two parties promising to do or not to do an action.

- **Quasi Contract:** -Quasi contacts are those that are implied by the laws. It is based on the principle that one should not enrich himself at the cost of other.

- **Implied Contact:** -In this contract, the action of one of the parties implies that completion of contract, even though it is not in writing.

- **Contingent Contract:** -It is defined as a contract to do or not to do something, if some event, collateral is attached to them.

Performance of Contracts:

A contract is said to be performed under the Indian Contract Act, 1872 when the rights and obligations created by the contract are fulfilled. Contracts are performed by any of the following actions: -

- By performance
- By tender
- By mutual consent or agreement
- By lapse of time
- By impossibility of performance
- By breach of contract
- By *force majeure* or an act of god.

Steps to Follow When Drawing Up Contracts:

The following 9 steps are required to follow when drawing up Contracts: -

- **Get it in writing:** The Hospitality and Hotel mangers needs to get all contracts in writing whenever or wherever possible. Also, as many a contract are complex in nature, it is advisable to have these contracts reviewed by an advocate from time to time for factual updates on specific or group of clauses.

- **Read the contract thoroughly:** There are many a Hospitality and Hotel Managers who sign a contract without thoroughly reading them up. An overhaul of a complete contract with an eye for detail is should be an important constituent of the operations. Further, at many times it is not possible for the Managers, staff to fulfill all of their contractual responsibilities due to constraints in operations.

- **Keep copies all contact documents:** It is important to keep a copy of all contacts that are signed. It will be better if abstracts note on the major or significant agreement clauses & then to file these notes. Many hospitality and hotel managers follow the best practices of keeping a separate section in their files devoted specially to these contracts.

- **Use good faith when negotiating contacts:** All hospitality and Hotel contracts need to have a good faith across both or all the parties of the said contract. A careful, realistic assessment of contract capability and capacity can go a long way in avoiding breach of contract.

- **Note & calendar time deadlines for performance:** When a contract requires specific actions to be taken by or on designated dates, it becomes important to list those specific dates in calendar form. This will lead to avoiding mistakes when the actual task is to be accomplished

- **Ensure the performance of third parties:** It is important to recognize that when the third-party requirement will arise, in order to ensure their optimum performance. This can be done by making an inclusive content of possible failures to perform in the third-party contract. ***Example:*** - In Hotel Industry, the Audio- Visual requirements by guests is mostly catered by third party vendor.

- **Share contract information with those who need to know:** Hospitality and Hotel Managers who have negotiated contracts, should share the information with their employees. This needs to be done, as the employees are the frontline staff who will enact to complete the process or essence of the contract.

- **Educate staff on the consequences of the breach of contract:** The employees at supervisory level and the Frontline staff of Core departments of Hotel and Hospitality operations needs to be educated and trained on the variations in policy with respect to specific or tailor-made contracts.

- **Resolve ambiguities as quickly and fairly as possible:** Despite the best intentions of both the parties of a contract, contractual problems can still arise. Whenever such situations arise, it is important for both or all parties of the contract agreement to be dealt compassionately and promptly.

Hospitality Contracts:

There are types of contract that are unique to Hotel operations, which are as follows: -

- **Group Information Sheet (GIS)**: It is a contract between the Hotel and Travel Agent or Online Travel Agent (OTA) which provides details like – Accommodation, Meal Plan & other miscellaneous services to be provided to the group.
- **Function Prospectus – Banquets**: The Function Prospectus (FP) is a signed contract between the hotel and the guests towards organizing and conducting a banquet event. It lists details of the event date, time, venue, type of function, Guaranteed Guests /, expected Guests / paxs, Rate charge per guests, Food and Beverage Menu, setup of venue, mode of settlement & any other special instructions.
- **Purchase Contract**: It specifies the goods or services that are required by the Hotel from a vendor for a specific period on agreed commercial terms. It indicates the quality parameters of the product or service, defining the place, time and period for the execution of this contract.
- **Franchisee Agreements**: A franchisee agreement is signed between the owners and the hotel franchising companies.
- **Management Contracts**: Management Contracts are entered by owners who either lack expertise of hotel operations or lack time to invest in hotel operations due to multiple reasons.
- **Technical Service Agreement (TSA)**: It is signed between the owner and the operator. Its formation is a part of the Management Contract. This agreement ensures the quality standards and specifications of the brand during construction of the Hotel.

Preventive Legal Management & Contract:

Breach of Contract: It is the failure to keep the promises or agreements of a contract. At times, it is next to impossible to fulfill the obligations set forth in a contract. Guests who stay past their previously agreed upon departure dates may make it difficult to honor upcoming Room reservations due to their overstay. Similar problems might exist in booking a table at the specialty restaurant.

Natural disaster, Man-made disasters like riots, strikes, civil disorder, and curtailment of transport services may make keeping up to the hospitality contract impossible. Voluntary breach of contract occurs when management elects to willfully violate the terms of the contract. When it is done, it means that the breaching party should not have agreed to the contract terms in the first place.

Preventing Breach of Contract: As a popular saying "Prevention is better than cure" is fully applicable in case of the Breach of contract. Breach of contract plays a vital role in the negative impact on both or all the parties of the contract. In many a case, the Hospitality Manager or Hotel Manager can avoid breaching contracts by following specific steps before and after entering into a contractual agreement. The following steps can help in preventing or minimizing the chance of litigation in future.

Remedies and Consequences of Breaching an Enforceable Contract: If a contract terms are broken, then the consequences of some of these breach contract can be very serious in nature. The plaintiff has multiple options when the other party has breached a contract. Some of the possible remedies are as follows:

i. Suit for specific performance

After the selection of this option, the party that broke the contract is taken to court with the plaintiff requesting for

- The court force the defendant to perform specific contract terms that have not been performed OR
- To refrain from engaging in some activity that is prohibited by the contract

ii. Liquidated damages

Breach of contract will call for a specific penalty. This happens when contract terms are not completed on an agreed date.

iii. Economic Loss

When damages have not been specially agreed upon in terms of the contact, the party that has breached the contract will still be held responsible for complete damages.

iv. Alternate dispute resolution

The two most common types of dispute resolution techniques are ***Arbitration*** and ***Mediation***. In Arbitration, the arbitrator is independent unbiased person who works with the contracting parties to understand their views. In Mediation, the unbiased independent person helps both the parties to come to a consensus on disputed activity.

Statute of Limitation: It is important to make optimum use of courts in order to enforce a contract in a timely manner. This is because, there are specific laws wherein, the maximum time period limit for courts to enforce contracts are clearly specified. These laws are known as Statute of

Limitation.

Indemnity and Guarantee: Indemnity can be defined as one of the parties agrees to pay the liabilities incurred by that specific party based on happening of an event. The guarantee is a form of security to be honored by the liability party.

Surety: -Surety is the person giving the guarantee. A surety can be discharged of its obligations in the following manner: -

- If any material change is done in the contract by the principal debtor and the creditor without the knowledge of the surety, the surety is discharged of his future obligations (Section133)
- Any contract that results in the release of the principal debtor by the creditor discharges the surety of his obligations (Section134)
- Any contract between the principal debtor and the creditor, where the creditor promises to give time or not to sue the principal debtor, discharges the surety of his obligations unless he agrees (Section135)
- If the creditor does an act that is inconsistent with the rights of a surety, or fails to do his duty to the surety as requested of him, resulting in the impairment of the surety's rights against the principal debtor the surety is discharged (Section139)

Bailment & Pledge

Bailment is the transfer of property without transfer of ownership. It can be non- gratuitous, gratuitous, voluntary, or involuntary. Pledge is the transfer of ownership and property to the payee. It is bailment done for a specific type of purpose, which is to secure a loan or to satisfy a debt.

Negotiable Instrument Act, 1881:

In Hotel operations, the financial transactions are to be related, so as to enable parties to effectively discharge their obligations under contracts. The Negotiable Instruments Act, 1881 and the Negotiable Instruments (Amendment and Miscellaneous Provisions) Act 2002 defines negotiable instruments and the process for their encashment.

Negotiable Instrument: Negotiable Instrument is a transferable signed document that promises to pay the bearer a sum of money at a future date or on demand and is transferable by way of delivery or by endorsement.

Types of Negotiable Instrument: Under Section 13 of the Negotiable Instrument Act, 1881, a negotiable instrument means a promissory note, bills of exchange or cheque payable either to order or to bearer.

HOTEL LICENSE AND REGULATIONS:

It is discussed under following sub sections:

- Introduction
- Two Stages of Hotel License
- Project Stage
- Operational Stage
- Boarding & Lodging License
- Food & Beverage Operations
- Personnel Department
- Accounts Department
- Banqueting and Catering Contracts
- Hotel / Motel Safety Act

Introduction:

The city planners incorporate Hotel and more largely tourism related activities like amusement parks, entertainment centers, convention centers Etc. in the planning stage. These components of planning stage are then incorporated into the bigger City Master Plan. This is mainly done, so stop enhances the foreign currency earnings & other Economic benefits. After, this Hotel Laws are monitored and regulated by central and state laws.

Two Stages of Hotel License:

Broadly, the development stages of Hotel Licenses are divided into two stages:

Project Stage: - In this stage, the Hotel requires Licenses &permissions from various government regulatory bodies prior to the commencement of their project. In certain cases, the Hotel will require Licenses and permissions during the construction phase of the project.

Operational Stage: - In this stage the Hotel requires Licenses and permissions required from various governments regulatory bodies during the closure of the project and in some cases during the commencement of hotel business operations.

Project Stage:

The Central and state governments of India from time to time announce various incentives towards construction of Hotels. Some of the major benefits that are given by the central and state governments are listed as follows: -

- The subsidy on capital investments in Hotel Projects (Land cost, cost of construction, plant &Machinery, equipment's Etc.)
- Sales-tax waiver for a period of 5 years from the date of commencement of Hotel operations or exemption from building or property tax.
- The newly constructed hotels enjoy a partial reimbursement of electrical expenses in first 5 years of operations.
- Land for construction of hotels can get a 25 percent subsidy against the acquisition cost.
- Under the Export Promotion Capital Goods (EPCG) scheme concessions in imports of equipment's for Hotel operations is granted.
- Subsidy up to 60 percent against the Insurance premium for the first two years

Operational Stage:

On completion of the Hotel building interiors, the Partial completion certificate (PCC) is converted to Completion Certificate by the municipal corporation. After this, stage the Hotel Company forwards an application for the Occupancy Certificate (OC) from the Municipal Corporation. The Municipal Corporation issues this certificate after the Hotel has obtained all permissions from the various government authorities.

Boarding & Lodging License:

This is issued by the Additional commissioner of police, Licensing Branch. It becomes mandatory requirement of the Hotel to collect relevant details of the guest at the time of Registration

Timeline for Boarding and Lodging License: - The Sarai Act (XXII of 1867)

Sarai:

Sarai means the provisions of the act is applicable on...

- Building used for the shelter and accommodation of travelers, and
- Cases in which only a part of the building is used for this accommodation.
- The place or building that is used for only night shelter by travelers (popularly, known as *Purao*).

Keepers of Sarai: -

The "Keepers of Sarai" means the owner and any person having or the Manager / supervisor acting in the care of management thereof.

Magistrate of the District: -

"Magistrate of the District" means of the in-charge chief officer of the provisional district in a civilian or criminal matter.

- He/ she provides updates of Sarai Act to the Sarai on a regular basis.
- He / she ensures that the Sarai Act is followed in documentation in form of Registrar.

Power to Order Reports from Keeper of Sarai:

The Magistrate of the district from time to time can order for the reports (either orally or written) from the keepers of Sarai.

Bye-Laws of Local Authorities:

In India, all commercial accommodation units are regulated as per the municipal regulations. The following are the bye-laws related to the regulation of hotels, lodging house, Heritage hotels and other supplementary commercial accommodations: -

- Act means the concerned city / area under Municipal Act.
- Licensee means a person is granted a license.

Rental Control Acts for Hotels & Lodging Houses:

- These are Acts to provide the control of rents and evictions.
- This includes the Rates, Tariffs of Hotel & Lodging industry.
- Lease of vacant commercial premises in the specified area is covered in this act.
- This act is otherwise known as Rent Control Act.

Export Promotion Capital Goods Scheme: -

The Export Promotion Capital Goods (EPCG) Scheme allows import or domestic sourcing of capital goods at 0.30 percent customs duty for all sectors as against the normal total of 25.852 percent. This means a duty saved to value of more than 25.55 percent of the import value. This duty saved I subject to an Export Obligation (EO) equivalent to six to eight times of the duty saved to be fulfilled in a period of 6 / 8/12 years from the date of issuance of the License.

Shop's and Establishment Act: - Registration of Hotels, Restaurants and other commercial catering establishments under the shop's and establishment Act is mandatory in nature.

Hotel Classification: - Hotels in India are classified from one star to five stars deluxe by the Department of Tourism. A Hotel must apply for classification within three months of its being operational.

NOC from Chief Fire Officer: - As each state in India frames its own fire safety & prevention laws. The Hotel in the resident state must take the approval of the Chief Fire officer of the town / city.

Restricted Money Changer's License: - Restricted Money Changer's License is issued by Reserve Bank of India to the Hotel. The Foreign currency received by guests through Encashment certificate is then given to the banks or full-fledged money changers.

Lift Operating License: License to operate a lift is given by the chief Inspector of Lifts.

NOC from Pollution Board: - The pollution control board after inspection of installed STP's, provision for rain water harvesting and DG will issue a NOC.

Permission to Install Signage and Hoardings: - The permission to Install Signage and Hoardings is given by municipal corporation.

Swimming Pool & Cooling Tower permission: - Swimming Pool & Cooling Tower is checked by the police and then permission is granted.

Food & Beverage Operations:

The Laws that effect the Production & service of Food & Beverage. These are commonly referred as —Food Laws —.

Health Trade License: - Generally, The Factories Act lays down conditions for safeguard towards health and safety of employees of organization. But, in case of Hotel Industry, Health Trade License is issued by the Directorate of Health Services to restaurant's, Eating Houses or other catering establishments

Eating House or Restaurant License: - The Restaurant License is issued by the police commissioner upon receiving the Health trade license.

Sanitary Certificate: - The Sanitary certificate is issued by the Health Department.

Liquor License: - The hotels require L-3 License for Room Service and L-5 License for Bars in star category hotels.

Nominations under the Food Safety and Standards Act, 2006: -

The Food Safety and Standards Act (FSSAI) has retained the nomination under section 17(2) and Rule 12-13 of the Prevention of Food Adulteration Rule 1955. This makes the Hotel's management mandatory to nominate Manager / Supervisor for day-to-day operations of Restaurant.

Certification of Weighing Scales and Peg Measures: - The Certification of Weighing Scales and Peg Measures is done under the FSSAI Act.

Personnel Department:

The Personnel Department is responsible for welfare activities of employees. This may involve activities like providing Provident Fund (PF) and Employee state Insurance Corporation (ESIC) authorities.

Labour Department Registration: The hotel register's with Labourdepartment. This registration requires the hotel to submit annual returns to the Labour office on the manpower strength of the hotel with minimum wages, date of payment & list of holidays under the National and Festival Holidays Act,1958.

Employee Provident Fund Registration: The Hotel has to Register itself with the Provident Fund commissioner's office under the Provident Fund Act,1952. This will lead to the Hotel obtaining the establishment code.

Employee State Insurance Scheme: Every Hotel register with the Employee Satiate Insurance (ESIC) Scheme under the Employee State Insurance Act,1948.

Professional Tax Enrolment Certificate: The Hotel deducts professional tax of employees(whose annual income is more than Rs. 5000 per annum) and deposits on their behalf. This deduction is on the basis of Maharashtra State Tax on Professionals, Trade, Callings and Employment Act. 1975.

Accounts Department:

The accounts department register's the Hotel with appropriate tax authorities and ensures that all statutory compliance is met from time to time.

Goods &Service Tax (GST)Registration: The Registration of all Hotel Property across different star classification has become mandatory in our country. A Unique GST Number is allocated to each of the Hotel property. The hospitality industry in the Indian economy, was liable to pay multiple taxes (VAT, luxury tax, and service tax) under the previous VAT regime. This is changed with a simplified Goods and Service Tax (GST). The hospitality sector stands to reap the benefits of standardized and uniform tax rates, and easy and better utilization of input tax credit.

Permanent Account Number: Permanent Account Number (PAN) Registration certificate is a 10- digit alphanumeric Identity card issued by the Income Tax Department. Each assesses whether individual, firm or company have unique PAN Registration.

Tax Information Network: Tax information network registration meets the requirement for e-filing of taxes records. These taxes filed can be checked by Accounts department.

Property Tax Certificate: Property Tax Certificate implies that the owners of the property regularly pay the property tax on time to time basis.

Banqueting and Catering Contracts:

The Hotel Industry follows the Contracts for their banquet functions in form of Function Prospectus (FP).Besides, the Menu, Pricing (in form of Advance deposit, Amount to be paid during the function and last payment after the function), Procedure of service, Date & time of Venue, Guaranteed and expected paxs (in hotel terminology persons to be catered are mentioned as paxs) other details of the contract are mentioned. In Standalone Food & Beverage outlets like Restaurants & Catering companies, this is known as Catering contracts.

Banqueting and Catering Contracts has been defined as the act of providing food and drinks on a given set of terms of contract. The range of responsibilities may involve delivery of meals, technical support or even full management of a restaurant. The contract that will be signed between the parties should disclose all material obligations to be involved in.

Event Details:

- The date, location, start time, and length of your event.
- If your venue has several banquet rooms or ballrooms, refer to your venue room by its specific name. For example, —The cocktail hour is to be held at The Front Street Hotel in the Grand Salon, followed by the reception at The Front Street Hotel on the Lakeview Terrace.

Cost Breakdown:

- The number of guests you expect at your event.
- The price per adult guest.
- The price per child guest and vendor.
- If you're hosting a buffet-style or tray-passed event, the method in which prices are determined: by the guest or the plate.
- The maximum market price you agree to pay for specialty items (i.e. lobster, crab, and fine fish).
- The total cost of rentals provided by your caterer.
- The estimated total cost for the reception.

Service and Staff:

- The ratio of bartenders and servers per guest.
- The name of the person overseeing the staff.
- The name of the party responsible for the event set up, clean up, and break down.
- The type of service you want (sit down, buffet, tray-passed, or some combination).
- The manner in which servers and bartenders will dress.
- The cost per hour or flat rate for servers/bartenders, including overtime costs.

The Menu:

- The number of courses served, including the cocktail hour, if applicable.
- The menu for each course, including acceptable substitutions should ingredients be unavailable.
- Any special arrangements needed for vegetarian or children‘s meals.
- Where and when you‘re to-go snack will be available.
- The wedding cake size, style, design, flavor, and cost, if applicable.
- The Groom‘s cake size, style, design, flavor and cost, if applicable.
- Any additional cake-cutting and service fees.
- The packaging of the wedding cake for guests to take home, if applicable.
- The preparation and freezing arrangement for the top tier of the wedding cake, if applicable.

Wine and Spirits:

- The types of alcohol that will be served.
- The times which each alcohol should be served (i.e., full bar for the cocktail hour, red and white wine during dinner, champagne for toasts and with dessert).
- Mixers, non-alcoholic beverages, and condiments you want included at your bar.
- Non-alcoholic beverages you want to serve during dinner, including coffee and tea.
- Corkage fees, if applicable.

- If you‘re supplying your own alcohol, when and where it should be delivered to the caterer.
- If you are buying alcohol from your caterer, cost per bottle/drink breakdown for wine, spirits, and non-alcoholic beverages.
- Your caterer‘s buyback policy. For example, if you ordered 75 bottles of wine, and opened only 50, the price at which your caterer will ―buy back‖ your unopened bottles.
- Additional costs for servers/bartenders who stay later than initially contracted for.
- Additional costs for rental delivery, set up, clean up, break down and return.

Policies and Procedures:

- Your caterer‘s proof of liability and insurance carrier information.
- The latest date you can make changes to your menu.
- The deposit amount paid.
- The balance due.
- The payment schedules.

The refund and cancellation policy. It‘s important to take the time to read through and fully understand your caterer‘s refund and cancellation policy. Example: - If you cancel your caterer‘s contract months before your event, will your deposit be refunded, or will you be charged for the outstanding balance.

Hotel / Motel Safety Act:

Introduction: The Hotel and Motel Fire Safety Act is to save lives and protect property by promoting fire and life safety in hotels, motels and other places of public accommodation. The law mandates that federal employees on travel must stay in public accommodations that adhere to the life safety requirements in the legislation guidelines. It also states that federally funded meetings and conferences cannot be held in properties that do not comply with the law.

Applicability of this Law: This law is applicable to all places of public accommodation, and requires that such properties are equipped with:

- Hard-wired, single-station smoke detectors in each guestroom

- Automatic sprinkler system (Components of an automatic fire sprinkler system. Typically, a Fire Sprinkler Systems are made up from a series of components including; Stop Valve, Alarm Valve, Fire Sprinkler (head), Alarm Test Valve and Motorized Alarm Bell), with a sprinkler head (A fire sprinkler or sprinkler head is the component of a fire sprinkler system that discharges water when the effects of a fire have been detected) in each guest room.
- Properties three stories or lower in height are exempt from the sprinkler requirement.

Fire extinguishers required on each floor. Every hotel shall provide each floor with one or more fire extinguishers of a type approved by the National Board of Fire Underwriters, which shall be kept in good working order at all times, with plain instructions thereon.

Stairways: All hotels over two stories in height and over one hundred feet in length shall be constructed so that there shall be at least two stairs for the use of guests leading from the ground floor to the uppermost story and for larger buildings.

Directions for reaching fire escapes: In every hotel having fire escapes directions for reaching the fire escapes shall be kept posted at the entrance of each stairway and elevator shaft and in each bedroom above the ground floor.

The Fire Precautions Act: The Fire Precautions Act lay down stipulations that the occupier of the premises must take into consideration, these were known as Interim Arrangements, the occupier, having made an application for a fire certificate, now had a duty to ensure that

- the means of escape can be safely and effectively used at all material times
- the means of firefighting are maintained in efficient working order, and
- all people employed to work in the premise should receive instructions and have training in what action to take in the event of a fire.

Restriction in Playing Recorded Music in Guest Room/ Public Areas: A license is required where music is being played in public, whether or not it is merely part of the ambience or an integral part of the atmosphere of a business. Just because a performance is given for free, the audience is small or the performance is confined to a small area, it does not mean the music is not being played in public. As mentioned earlier, it is immaterial that you own a copy of the recording. Without an appropriate license, you only have the right to use these things privately or domestically.

Restriction on playing music in the public area or guest room:

- The permission for playing loud music in public area or in rooms of the hotel which disturbs the guest is not allowed.
- Music should be within 124 decibels.
- Special permission is to be taken under law for playing music in loud speakers in residential area post 10 p.m.

HOTEL INSURANCE:

Hotel insurance is discussed under following sub-sections:

- Introduction
- The Indian Contracts Act, 1987
- Principles of Insurance Contract
- Purchasing an Insurance Policy
- Types of Insurance Policy
- Insurance Coverage in Hotel Industry
- Filling an Insurance Claim
- Grievances Redressal Machinery

Introduction:

The Insurance industry in India is built on four fundamental premises: -

Actuary Method: - The Insurance companies use this method when, clearing of claims comes in large or uncontrolled numbers. The data for claims is arranged as per statisticians use of Actuary method. This method helps to predict the average frequency of loss involved in the risk.

The monetary value of the loss must be calculated on the basis of accepted standards

The **premium fees** for the insurance must be low in value. This will in turn help in attracting new customers who seek to be **insured**.

The risk must not have the possibility of occurring very frequently during any given time period. This will make the insurer pay for all legitimate claims on regular basis.

The Indian Contracts Act, 1987

The Indian Contracts Act,1987 states that Insurance is a contract of indemnity between two persons – the indemnifier (Insurance Company) and the indemnified (insured) towards the reimbursement of a loss. The liability of the indemnifier (Insurance company) is primary and arises when the event occurs.

Principles of Insurance Contract:

The Principles of Insurance are applied by Insurance companies when they have to interpret the terms and conditions as stated in the Insurance policy. This Principe is applied during the process of an insurance claim. The Most commonly applied principles of Insurance Contracts are as follows; -

Principle of Utmost Good Faith: The Principle of Utmost Good Faith states that the needs to be in form of full disclosure with all relevant material by both the parties – The Insurer and the Insured Party.

Principles of Indemnity: It implies that the loss amount shall be paid to the extent of the policy provided if all the premiums are fully paid up as on the date of the incident. When computing the loss, two methods are used - **Actual Cash Method** & **Fair Market value**

Principles of Subrogation: This is invoked when a third party is responsible for the loss. It can be applied only when the claim is fully paid up.

Principle of Insurable Interest: According to this principle, the legal right to insurance arises out of a financial relationship between the insured and the subject matter of Insurer. Also, without an Insurable Interest, Insurers will not cover the loss.

Principle of Contribution: According to the Principle of Contribution, the indemnity provided for the loss occurring on the asset, which is insured with several insurer's has to be proportionately shared among themselves. The sharing proportion should be in accordance to the ratable proportion of the loss.

Principle of proximate cause: It relates to the immediate cause of the mishap that resulted in the loss. It establishes a relation between action and the result. The result may be in the form of injury or loss of items.

Purchasing an Insurance Policy:

The customers should understand the implications of the insurance before actually taking up an insurance policy. The purchase of Insurance policy can be through Insurance agent, Insurance broker or over the internet by online registration. In most cases a policy should be taken through an Insurance broker, as he/she will provide in depth analysis for every stages of the Insurance policy. The benefits and costs involved with riders are better explained by an Insurance broker in comparison with others.

Types of Insurance Policy:

Insurance can be broadly classified into four stages: -

- Life Insurance
- General Insurance
- Fire Insurance
- Marine Insurance

Also, the Fire and Marine Insurance policies are issued by the General Insurance Companies. The policies of Life Insurance or General Insurance can be further categorized as per the Individual or the Company.

Insurance Coverage in Hotel Industry:

The Hotel Companies have to protect Plant, Machinery, Furniture &Fixtures, other Physical assets, Guests, employee's and from third party liabilities claims. The third-party liability claims are mainly due to

- Deficiency in service
- Not delivering upon promises
- Injuries sustained by guest's during their stay at the Hotel Premises
- Injuries sustained by guest's using any of the Hotel facilities

Some of the insurance policies listed in the Hotel companies are as follows: -

- Machinery breakdown policy
- Standard fire policy
- Electronic equipment's
- Boiler and pressure plant
- Cash in safe
- Cash in transit
- Cash in Counter
- Plate glass insurance
- Group health insurance
- Fleet insurance policy
- Workmen compensation insurance
- Fidelity guarantees policy

- Neon sign insurance
- Loss of profit insurance
- Public liability Insurance

Filling an Insurance Claim:

The Hotel Management needs to understand the process of Insurance claim settlement. This will help the Hotel Management to plan the timeline for the reinstatement of the property. There are three stages for processing Insurance claims. These are –

- Initial Stage
- Investigate Stage
- Settlement Stage

Initial Stage: In this stage, the information has to be sent to the insurance company at the earliest. After this, the insurance company internally initiates the claim procedure.

Investigate Stage: This stage involves the appointment of a surveyor or loss assessor by the Insurance company. The claim is processed on the basis of: -

- The completed claim forms
- Independent reports from the surveyors, legal or medical opinion.
- The document furnished by the insured.

Settlement Stage: Once the claim is in order, settlement is affected by cheque. Once the insurance claim amount is finalized, the hotel can commence the repair and restoration work, subject to final disbursement by the insurance company.

Grievances Redressal Machinery:

When the Insurance company fails to deliver on its promise, Hotel companies can approach Institutions for the redressal of their complaints.

Institution of Insurance Ombudsman: The Institution of Insurance Ombudsman was set up in year 1999 under the section 114 (1) of InsuranceAct,1938. Prior to approaching the insurance Ombudsman for redressal of consumer grievance redressal officer. The ombudsman hears complaints related to –

- Delay in settlement of claim
- Rejection of Insurance claim
- Partial settlement of claims
- Non- settlement of claims

Loss Prevention Association of India: Loss Prevention Association of India was setup under the General Insurance Corporation of India with aim of promoting safety and loss prevention through education, training, advertisement Etc.

SUMMARY:

Business option for foreign Investors in India :- The business options available for foreign investors or foreign companies desirous of doing business in India are Sole Proprietor, Partnership Firm, Limited Liability Partnership (LLP) firms, Private Limited Company, Public Limited Company, Liaison Office, Representative Office, Project Office, Branch Office, Wholly-owned Subsidiary Company & Joint Venture (JV) Company.

Foreign Exchange Management Act, 1999: -Foreign Exchange Regulation Act (FERA) was incorporated in 1973 with the objective of Regulating foreign business in India, maintaining exchange Rate Stability & Conserving & cushioning foreign exchange reserves Regulatory issues that affect the Hotel business environment are classified into the Direct Taxes and Indirect Taxes.

The different types of contract seen in hotel industry are Bilateral Contract, Unilateral Contract, Express Contract, Quasi Contract, Implied Contact and Contingent Contract The 9 steps that are required to follow when drawing up Contracts are Get it in writing , Read the contract thoroughly , Keep copies all contact documents , Use good faith when negotiating contacts , Note & calendar time deadlines for performance , Ensure the performance of third parties , Share contract information with those who need to know , Educate staff on the consequences of the breach of contract and Resolve ambiguities as quickly and fairly as possible. Remedies of Breaching an Enforceable Contract are Suit for specific performance, Liquidated damages, Economic Loss & Alternate dispute resolution. Broadly, the development stages of Hotel Licenses are divided into Project Stage & Operational Stage.

Restricted Money Changer's License: - Restricted Money Changer's License is issued by Reserve Bank of India to the Hotel. The Foreign currency received by guests through Encashment certificate is then given to the banks or full-fledged money changers.

Food Laws: -The Laws that effect the Production & service of Food & Beverage.

Liquor License: - The hotels require L-3 License for Room Service and L-5 License for Bars in star category hotels.

Employee Provident Fund Registration: -The Hotel has to Register itself with the Provident Fund commissioner's office under the Provident Fund Act, 1952. This will lead to the Hotel obtaining the establishment code.

Employee State Insurance Scheme: -Every Hotel register with the Employee Satiate Insurance (ESIC) Scheme under the Employee State Insurance Act, 1948.

Professional Tax Enrolment Certificate: -The Hotel deducts professional tax of employees (whose annual income is more than Rs. 5000 per annum) and deposits on their behalf. This deduction is on the basis of Maharashtra State Tax on Professionals, Trade, Callings and Employment Act. 1975.

Goods & Service Tax (GST) Registration: -The Registration of all Hotel Property across different star classification has become mandatory in our country. A Unique GST Number is allocated to each of the Hotel property.

Permanent Account Number: - Permanent Account Number (PAN) Registration certificate is a 10- digit alphanumeric Identity card issued by the Income Tax Department. Each assesses whether individual, firm or company have unique PAN Registration.

Property Tax Certificate: -Property Tax Certificate implies that the owners of the property regularly pay the property tax on time to time basis. Insurance can be broadly classified into Life Insurance, General Insurance, Fire Insurance & Marine Insurance the three stages for processing Insurance claims are Initial Stage, Investigate Stage & Settlement Stage

GLOSSARY:

Memorandum of Association: The Memorandum of Association is a document that sets the constitution of the company and defines the relationship of the company with outside world.

Articles of Association: The Articles of Association lays down the rules and regulations for the internal management of the company for achieving the objectives stated in the Memorandum of Association.

Foreigner's Regional Registration Office: Under the Foreigner's Act 1946 and Registration of Foreigner's Act, 1939; hotels need to furnish required details of all foreigners to the Foreigner's Regional Registration Office (FRRO) & Bureau of Immigration

Corporate Tax: It is the tax payable by the Hotel Company on its income acquired over the just concluded financial Year. For the purpose of taxation, Hotel companies are categorized as either domestic or foreign companies, A public or private limited company or Management Control based company from the Indian sub-continent.

Transfer Pricing: Then laws relating to Transfer pricing was introduced in 2001 through 92A to 92F of the Income Tax Act, 1961. The purpose of the law was to ensure that the dealings are between two group companies or an Associated Enterprises (AE) located across borders followed by Arm's Length (ALP).

Indian Contract Act, 1872: The purpose of the Indian Contract Act, 1872 was to introduce certainty to a transaction. It also voices the principles that make an agreement into a legally enforceable contract.

Arbitration and **Mediation**: In Arbitration, the arbitrator is independent unbiased person who works with the contracting parties to understand their views. In Mediation, the unbiased independent person helps both the parties to come to a consensus on disputed activity.

Indemnity and Guarantee: Indemnity can be defined as one of the parties agrees to pay the liabilities incurred by that specific party based on happening of an event. The guarantee is a form of security to be honored by the liability party.

Bailment & Pledge: Bailment is the transfer of property without transfer of ownership. It can be non- gratuitous, gratuitous, voluntary, or involuntary. Pledge is the transfer of ownership and property to the payee. It is bailment done for a specific type of purpose, which is to secure a loan or to satisfy a debt.

Negotiable Instrument Act, 1881: In Hotel operations, the financial transactions are to be related, so as to enable parties to effectively discharge their obligations under contracts. The Negotiable Instruments Act, 1881 and the Negotiable Instruments (Amendment and Miscellaneous Provisions) Act 2002 defines negotiable instruments and the process for their encashment.

The Indian Contracts Act, 1987: The Indian Contracts Act, 1987 states that Insurance is a contract of indemnity between two persons – the indemnifier (Insurance Company) and the indemnified (insured) towards the reimbursement of a loss. The liability of the indemnifier (Insurance Company) is primary and arises when the event occurs.

THREE

PUBLIC HEALTH AND SAFETY LAWS

INTRODUCTION:

The Labor laws in India focuses on employee-employer relations, with emphasis on employee welfare and benefits, settlement of grievances and Industrial disputes. The Hospitality law en-complates on the legal obligations of the hotelier in providing service and meeting guest requirements 24/7 X 365. We also contemplate on what the hotelier expects from an ideal guest.

INTRODUCTION TO LABOUR LAWS:

The laws that affect the employees of sell levels of operations who work in these organizations. Labour legislation in India started 150 years ago with the Apprentices Act, 1850. Labour laws in India is categorized by the Ministry of Labour according to the purpose that they have been enacted for. The Labour laws pursue the following two major categorization:

- Labour laws defining the relationship between employers, employees, and trade unions
- Labour Laws that provide rights of employees at workplace.

Overview of Labour Laws & Regulations:

There was many an act that followed this Act. But, since year 1960, the following Acts were implemented –

- In year 1961, Indian Standard s Institution (Certification Marks) Amendment Act.

- In year 1969, Monopolies and Restrictive Trade Practice Act
- In year 1977, Standards of weights and Measures (Packed Commodities) Rules.
- In year 1980, Prevention of Black Marketing and Maintenance of Suppliers of Essential Commodities Act.

Categorization of labour Laws:

The Categorization of Labour laws are further broken down as follows: -

Laws related to industrial Relations

- The Trade Unions Act, 1926
- The Industrial Employment Act, 1946
- The Trade Unions Act, 2001

Laws related to wages

- The Payment Wages Act, 1936
- The Minimum Wages Act, 1948
- The Payment of Bonus Act, 1965
- The Payment of Wages Act, 2005

Laws related to working hours, conditions of services, and employment

- The Factories Act, 1948
- The Contract Labour Act, 1970
- The Shops and Establishment Act, 1948

Laws related to equality and empowerment of women

- The Maternity Benefit Act, 1961
- The Equal Remuneration Act, 1976

Laws related to social security

- The Worker's Compensation Act, 1923
- The Employees State Insurance Act, 1948
- The Employees Provident Fund & Miscellaneous Provisions Act, 1952
- The Payment of Gratuity Act, 1972

- The Employees Provident Fund & Miscellaneous Provisions Act, 1996
- The Workmen's Compensation Act, 2000
- The Payment of Gratuity Act, 2010

Laws related to employment and training

- The Employment Exchanges Act, 1959
- The Apprentices Act, 1961

Laws related to employment and training

- The Weekly Holiday Act, 1942
- The Personal Injuries Act, 1963
- The Public Liability Insurance Act, 1991

The areas covered by Labour legislation are Working Conditions, Welfare, Health & Safety &Payments. Employees are classified into three categories.

Classification of Employees:

Employees are classified into three categories as illustrated in the above diagram.

- Government employees, civil servants and public servants are governed by the service conditions and rules that come from the Indian Constitution. These employees enjoy statutory protection of tenure of service and automatic pay increase as per designated scales.
- Public sector employees serving in government controlled organizations are governed by the service conditions of their own organizations.
- Private Sector employees are further divided into Management and staff.

TRADE UNION:

It is discussed under following sub-sections:

- Trade Union (definition)
- The Trade Union Act, 1926 and the Trade Unions (Amendments) Act, 2001
- Statutory compliances to be met by trade Unions
- Labour Laws that provide for Rights of Employees at Workplace
- Factories Act, 1948

Trade Union (definition):

A Trade Union is a voluntary organization of workers pertaining to a particular industry that is formed to balance and improve the relations between employers and employees in form of protection, welfare schemes, interest and collective action of workers.

The Trade Union Act, 1926 and the Trade Unions (Amendments) Act, 2001

This voluntary organization represents legitimate demands of the workers to Management and imbibe a sense of discipline and responsibilities in worker.

The administration of the Act is entrusted with the Ministry of Labour. Its tasks are as follows: -

- To monitor Industrial Relations at the Central Level
- Intervention, Mediation and conciliation of Industrial disputes
- Intervention in situations of threatened strikes and Lock-outs
- Implementation of settlement and Awards

Statutory compliances to be met by trade Unions:

The Statutory compliances that have to meet by the trade unions are as follows: -

- Registration of Membership
- Income and Expenses Statement
- Details of all Assets and Liabilities
- Statement of the General Fund and the political fund accounts
- Statement of Expenses made from the General Fund
- Availability of the Register of Membership and its Books of Accounts for inspection by the members of the Union

Labor Laws that provide for Rights of Employees at Workplace:

The Laws that Provide for Rights of Employees at Workplace are -

- Employment Exchanges Act, 1959
- The Apprentices Act, 1961
- Shops & Establishment Act, 1948
- The Minimum wages Act, 1948
- The Payment of Wages Act, 2005

- Equal Remuneration Act, 1976
- The Payment of Bonus Act, 1965
- Employees Provident Fund Scheme (EPF), 1952
- The Public Provident Act, 1968
- Weekly Holidays Act, 1942
- The Maternity Benefit Act, 1961
- The Worker's Compensation Act, 2000

Factories Act, 1948:

It contains provisions of Health, safety, welfare of worker's inside the factories, the hours of work, the minimum age of worker's and leave rules. The Act authority's periodic inspection by the Chief Inspector.

THE AREAS COVERED UNDER LABOUR LEGISLATION:

The areas covered by Labor legislation are: -

- Working Conditions
- Welfare
- Health & Safety
- Payments

Working Condition:

The Shop and Establishment Act covers the working conditions to be provided to all employees in Hotel and catering establishments. The working conditions of employees means –

- Fixation of working hours
- Regular and timely payment of wages
- Paid leave
- Creation of healthy working environment through basic necessities.

Unfair Labour Practices:

During the 18th and 19th Century in India, Indentured labour or bounded labour was supplied to the plantation owners by contractors, who in turn, provided Food &Accommodation to the Laboure's. This practice of providing indentured labour to the indigo plantation industry in Bengal and the Tea industry in Assam, laid the foundation of Labour legislations by the then British Imperial Rule in India.

Prohibition of unfair labour practice:

No employer or workman or a trade union, whether registered under the Trade4 Unions Act, 1926 or not, shall commit any unfair labour practice.

Penalty for illegal strikes and lock-outs:

Any workman who commences continues or otherwise acts in furtherance of, a strike which is illegal under this Act, shall be punishable with imprisonment for a term which may extend to one month, or with fine which may extend to fifty rupees, or with both.

Any employer who commences continues, or otherwise acts in furtherance of a lock- out which is illegal under this Act, shall be punishable with imprisonment for a term which may extend to one month, or with fine which may extend to one thousand rupees, or with both.

Penalty for instigation:

Any person who instigates or incites others to take part in, or otherwise acts in furtherance of, a strike or lock-out which is illegal under this Act, shall be punishable with imprisonment for a term which may extend to six months, or with fine which may extend to one thousand rupees, or with both.

Penalty for giving financial aid to illegal strikes and lock-outs:

Any person who knowingly expends or applies any money indirect furtherance or support of any illegal strike or lock-out shall be punishable with imprisonment for a term which may extend to six months, or with fine which may extend to one thousand rupees, or with both.

Welfare:

The factories Act 1948 covers the obligations of employers with respect to comfort and welfare facilities of staff. The provision of welfare to employees to be provided by employer includes –

- Washing facilities to staff
- First-Aid facilities
- Paid Annual Leave
- Uniforms including footwear
- Working hours not exceeding 10.5 hours a day and 48 hours a week. There needs to be provision for overtime.
- Paid Annual Leave at the rate of one-month salary for every year of service.
- **Housing Facilities**: - Besides providing semi-furnished house, some hotel companies provide facilities in form of House Rent Allowance (HRA). The HRA will be in proportion of the employee's salary.

- **Financial and Legal Services**: - This is with respect to offering loan facilities for various personal reasons of employees. Legal advice may be provided to enhance morale of the people.
- **Purchasing Services**: - Employer's provide scheme's, wherein the employees can purchase monthly groceries at discounted prices.
- **Recreational Activities**: - This activity is tailor made and are as per requirements of employees. The sole aim being physical and mental diversion of work.

Working Relations:

The Industrial Disputes Act, 1947 has provisions for good working relations through free communication and informal negotiations between people at work.

Health & Safety:

Health & safety looks into implementation of good environment practices in eco-friendly hotels. In India, the government has initiated Legislative measures to preserve the environment. This has led to successful waste management programme. Lastly, these all have impacted our lives.

Payments:

Payments are made by employers to staff in lieu of work done. The work may be in the form of wages, bonus, Insurance premium, Provident Fund, Gratuity payments & compensation of injury. The compensation Act, Employers State Insurance Act, 1948 and Minimum Wages Act, 1948 prevent employer's exploiting employees.

Payment of Wages Act, 1936:

The Payment of Wages Act, 1936 is one of the old enactments dealing with employer- employee relationship. The limited purpose of the Act is to ensure prompt and full payment of wages to persons employed in industry. The State of Maharashtra has extended the provisions of the Act to all establishments covered by the Bombay Shops and Establishments Act, 1948.

Penalties for Non-Compliance: Penalties prescribed are from Rs. 1,500-7,500. Repeat offences attract 1 to 6 months imprisonment and fine from Rs. 3,750-22,500. Delayed wage payments attract penalty of Rs. 750 per day of delay.

THE MINIMUM WAGES ACT, 1948 (DETAILED EXPLANATION):

A Minimum Wages Bill was introduced in the Central Legislative Assembly on 11.04.1946 and came into force with effect from 15.03.1948. The Committee on Fair Wage was set up in 1948 to provide guidelines for wage structure.

INTRODUCTION: The minimum wages Act 1948, was to secure the welfare of unorganized workers in certain industries by fixing the minimum rates of wages. The Act contemplates that minimum wages rates must ensure for him not only his subsistence and that of his family but also preserve his efficiency as a workman. The Act empowers the appropriate Government for fixation of minimum wages in employments enumerated in the schedule to the Act. The fixation of minimum wages relates to the industries where sweated labour is most prevalent or where there is inevitable chance of exploitation. In prescribing the minimum wages rates, the capacity of the employers needs to be considered as the State assumes that every employer must pay the minimum wages if he employs labor.

Interpretation/Definition (sec.2)

(a) **_Adult', _Adolescent' and _Child'** Adult- is who has completed his eighteen years of age. Adolescent – completed his fifteen years but not eighteen years of age. Child –who has not completed his fifteen years of age.

(b) **Appropriate government India** has federal form of Government at the center and state level. The minimum wages act provides separate areas of jurisdiction for both center and state government.

(c) **Employer** means any person who employs one or more employees in any schedule of employment.

(d) **Wages** means all remuneration capable of being expressed in terms of money.

(e) **Employee** means any person employed for hire or reward and includes an out –worker.

APPLICABILITY: It extends to the whole of India and applies to scheduled employments in respect of which minimum rates of wages have been fixed under this act.

Short title and extent (sec. 1):

- This Act, the Minimum Wages Act, 1948 extends to the whole of India.
- This Act may be called the Minimum Wages Act, 1948.

SCHEDULED EMPLOYMENTS: An employment specified in the schedule, or any process or branch of work forming part of such employment (Section-2g)

Recruitment of Employees Employment Exchange Act, 1959

- The Directorate General of Resettlement & Employment formulated the Employment Exchange Act.
- The Government of India has been publishing weekly magazine – Rozgaar Samachar or Employment News that lists all advertise vacancies.

  - The Institute of Hotel management & Catering Technology (IHMCT&AN), Food Corporation of India (FCI), Travel Association of India (TAAI), Indian association of Tour Operators (IATO) have agreement with Government & National Skill Development Corporation (NSDC) for _Hunar Se Rozgar Scheme' to provide skill-based jobs in Hospitality & Tourism sector.

Hiring of contractual employees

The Contract labour Act., 1970 and the Contract Labour Regulation Rules

A Contract's duties and responsibilities under this Act are: -

- To maintain the employees master Roll, Register of Wages, deductions, Overtime, Fines, Advances & Wages Slip [Rule 79]
- To display an abstract of the contract labour act with Rules in English, Hindi and Local Language [Rule 80]
- To display notices showing Rates of wages, Hours of Work, Wage Period, dates of Payment, Name and Address of the Inspector [Rule 81]

Duties & Liabilities of Hotelier's Under this Act

- Hotels should check whether the Contractor is registered and licensed under the Contract labour Act and the Contract Labour Regulation Rules before awarding the contract.
- Hoteliers are required to provide Canteen, Restroom, Drinking Water Facilities, Latrines and Urinals, Washing Facility & First Aid to contract employees.
- Hotels can make deductions in payment from contractor on offering facilities to its contracting employees.

FIXING OF MINIMUM RATES OF WAGES:

- The appropriate government shall fix the minimum rates wages payable to employees employed in a scheduled employment.

- Review at such intervals not exceeding five years, the minimum rates of wages so fixed and revise the minimum rates if necessary. The minimum rates of wages may be fixed as a minimum time rate or a minimum piece rate or as a guaranteed time rate (Section-3).

- Government can also fix Minimum Wages for

- **Time work:** Time Rate System: Under this system, the worker is paid by the hour, day, week, or month.
- **Piece work:** at piece rate Straight piecework system : The wages of the worker depend upon his output and rate of each unit of output; it is in fact independent of the time taken by him. Piece work for the purpose of securing to such employees on a time work basis
- **Overtime work** done by employees for piece work or time rate workers

Fixing of minimum rates of wages (sec.3):

- The minimum rates of wages will be reviewed/ revised, for every five years, by the appropriate govt.
- Appropriate govt. can add any employment, to the schedule (part-I or part – II), wherein one thousand or more employees are found working
- Different minimum rates of wages may be fixed for different scheduled employments/ different classes of work /different localities

Minimum rates of wages (Sec.4):

- Basic + Special Allowance (Which varies with the cost of living index -- a theoretical price index that measures relative cost of living over time or regions. It is an index that measures differences in the price of goods and services).
- Basic + Cash value of concessional supply of materials like food, clothes, etc.
- An all-inclusive rate which includes Basic + Cost of living Allowance + Cash value of concessional supply of materials.

Procedure for fixation and revision of minimum rates of wages (sec.5):

- **Publish** its proposals in the **official gazette** asking comments from the affected parties.

- Constitute **committees/sub committees** for the purpose.

- The committees/sub-committees and advisory boards constituted by the Government consist of equal number of members of:

  - Employers
  - Employees, and
  - Independent persons

FIXATION OF MINIMUM WAGES:

Advisory board (sec.7):

Appointed by appropriate government. - To co-ordinate the work of committees and sub committees appointed under Section 5.

Central advisory board (sec.8):

To advise the **Central and State Governments** in fixation and revision of minimum rates of wages. **&**to co-ordinate the work of the Advisory Boards.

Composition of Committees, etc. (Sec. 9):

Each of the committee, sub-committee and the Advisory Board shall consist of:

- persons to be nominated by the appropriate Government.
- representing the employers and employees in the scheduled employments who shall be equal in number and
- independent persons not exceeding one-third of its total number of members: one of such independent persons shall be appointed the Chairman by the appropriate Government.

PAYMENT OF MINIMUM WAGES:

Wages in kind (sec. 11):

- Minimum wages shall be **paid in cash**.
- The appropriate govt. may authorize, where there has been a **custom** of payment in this manner, payment of minimum wages either **wholly or**

partly in kind.

- The appropriate govt. may authorize supply of **essential commodities** at concessional rates.

PAYMENT OF MINIMUM RATES OF WAGES:

The employer shall pay to every employee in a scheduled employment under him wages at the rate not less than the minimum rates of wages fixed **under the Act. (Section-12)**

Payment of minimum rate of wages (sec. 12):

- The Minimum Wages has to be paid **without any deductions** other than Statutory Deductions.
- Payment of **wages less than minimum wages** on the ground of less performance or output is **illegal.**

HOURS OF WORK, OVERTIME:

The Act also provides for regulation or working hours, overtime, weekly holidays and overtime wages. Period and payment of wages, and deductions from wages are also regulated. **(Section—13 to 17)**

Fixing hours of work (sec. 13):

For an Adult Worker working in Factories:

- Number of Working Hours should not exceed **48 Hours** in a week with a
- Weekly Holiday.
- The Daily Hours should not exceed more than **9 Hours** with **1 Hour Rest Interval.**
- Provision of Compensatory Holiday/Overtime Wages if working on holiday.

Overtime wages (sec. 14):

- If the person has worked for more than 48 hours in a week then, the excess hours worked will be treated as Overtime.
- Overtime wage rate will be twice of the normal wage rate.

Wages for a person who has worked less than normal working hours (sec. 15):

- Employer could not provide the activities of the job then; the employee is entitled to receive full salary.
- Employee has not worked due to his unwillingness then; the employee is not entitled to receive full salary.

CLAIMS UNDER THE ACT (Section-20):

This section makes provisions to appoint authorities to hear and decide all claims arising out of payment less than the minimum rates of wages or any other monetary payments due under the Act. **The presiding officers of the Labour court and Deputy Labour Commissioners are the authorities appointed.**

In fixing or revising minimum rates of wages under this section:

- different minimum rates of wages may be fixed for-

- different scheduled employment
- different classes of work in the same scheduled employment
- adults, adolescents, children and apprentices
- different localities

- minimum rates of wages may be fixed by any one or more of the following wage- periods namely:

- by the hour,
- by the day,
- by the month, or
- by such other large wage-period as may be prescribed; and where such rates are fixed by the day or the month, the manner of calculating wages for a month or for a day, as the case may be, may be indicated.

Claims (sec. 20):

- A **Labour Commissioner** or any other appointed authority is authorized to hear claims regarding **non-payment of minimum wages**
- Any aggrieved person may **apply** to the authority for settling his claims
- within 6 months

Penalties (sec. 22):

- **Offence** - Payment of less than Minimum Wages to employee
- **Punishment** -Imprisonment which may extend up to 6 Months or Fine which may extend up to Rs 500/- or Both

WHO CAN FILE A CLAIM PETITION:

- The Employee or
- Any legal practitioner or any official of a regd. Trade union authorized in writing to act on his behalf or
- Any Inspector or
- Any person acting with the permission of the authority under Section-20 (I)

REGISTERS AND RECORDS:

Every employer shall maintain the following registers and records as required under the act

I. Register of wages **in Form No. XI or Form XII**

A muster-roll (collective or combined) **in Form No. VI**

Register of fines, **Form No. I**

Register of deductions for damage or loss in **Form No. II**

Register of overtime in **Form No. V**

Visit book

A wage slip in **Form No. XIII** shall be issued by every employer to every person employed by him at least a day prior to the disbursement of wages.

Records to be maintained (sec. 18):

The Registers should contain the following particulars-

(I) particulars of employed persons

- the work performed by them
- the wages paid to them
- the receipts given by them

NOTICE TO BE EXHIBITED:

A notice in Form IV containing the minimum rates of wages fixed together with the abstract of the Act, the rates made there under and the name and address of the inspector shall be displayed in English and in a language understood by the majority of the workers.

ANNUAL RETURNS:

Annual returns in Form III or Form III a as per rule 21 (4) (iii) shall be submitted to the Inspector before the first day of the February of the succeeding year.

PRESERVATION OF REGISTERS:

All the registers shall be preserved for a period of three years after the date of last entry made within.

PENALTY:

Any employer who contravenes (violates) any of the provisions of this Act other than those relating to Section 12 and 13 of any rules or any order made there under shall be punishable with fine, which may extend to Rs.500. Any employer who contravenes the provision relating to the payment of minimum rates of wages fixed (Section- 12) hours of work stipulated for constituting a normal working day as per section 13 shall be punishable with imprisonment for a term which may extend to six months or with fine which may extend to Rs. 500/- or with both.

Penalties (sec. 22):

- **Offence** - Payment of less than Minimum Wages to employee
- **Punishment** -Imprisonment which may extend up to 6 Months or Fine which may extend up to Rs 500/- or Both

AUTHORITIES APPOINTED UNDER THE ACT:

Inspector: (Under Section-19):

a. Labour Commissioner
b. Additional Labour Commissioner (IR and E)
c. Regional Joint Labour Commissioners
d. Joint Labour Commissioner (P)
e. Chief Inspector of Plantations
f. Deputy Labour Commissioner (HQ)
g. Dist. Labour Officer (HQ)
h. Additional Labour Commissioner, Kozhikode
a. Dist. Labour Officers (E)
j. Inspector of plantations
k. Asst. Labour Officers – Grade II

Claim Authorities (under Section –20):

- Labour Courts
- Deputy Labour Commissioners

Claims (sec. 20):

- A **Labour Commissioner** or any other appointed authority is authorized to hear claims regarding **non-payment of minimum wages**
- Any aggrieved person may **apply** to the authority for settling his claims within 6 months

Sanctioning Authority under Sec. 22:

- Labour Courts
- The chief inspector of plantations
- Dist. Labour officers

Penalties (sec. 22):

- **Offence** - Payment of less than Minimum Wages to employee
- **Punishment** -Imprisonment which may extend up to 6 Months or Fine which may extend up to Rs 500/- or Both

Contracting out (Sec. 25):

Any **contract or agreement**, whether made before or after the commencement of this Act, whereby an employee either relinquishes or **reduces his right to a minimum rate of wages** or any privilege or concession accruing to him under this Act shall be **null and void** so far as it purports to reduce the minimum rate of wages fixed under this Act.

Power of State Government to add schedule (sec.27):

- The State Government has to **notify** in the Official Gazette **not less than three months** of its intention to do so.

- **Power of Central Government to give directions (sec.28):** The Central Government may give directions to a State Government as to the carrying into execution of this Act in the State.

- **Penalties for Non-Compliance:** Imprisonment up to 6 months and/or fine up to Rs. 500 is imposable for contravention.

OTHER LABOUR LEGISLATIONS IN INDIA:

The other labour legislations in India is discussed under following sub-sections:

- Payment of Bonus Act, 1965
- Employee's Compensation Act, 1923
- Payment of Gratuity Act, 1972
- Employees Provident Funds & Miscellaneous Provisions Act, 1952
- Bombay Shops & Establishment Act, 1948
- Employees State Insurance Act, 1948
- Contract Labour (Regulations & Abolitions) Act, 1970
- Laws related to Equality and Empowerment of Women
- Sexual Harassment of Employees
- The Equal Remuneration Act, 1976
- Employees with Special Needs
- Employee Safety at the Workplace
- Employees' State Insurance Act, 1948

Payment of Bonus Act, 1965:

The Payment of Bonus Act, 1965, gives to the employees a statutory right to a share in the profits of his employer. The Act enables the employees to get a minimum bonus equivalent to one month's salary or wage (8.33% of annual earnings) whether the employer makes profit or not. But the Act also puts a ceiling on the Bonus and the maximum bonus payable under the Act is equivalent to 2½ months' salary or wage (20% of annual earnings).

Penalties for Non-Compliance: Imprisonment up to 6 months and/or fine up to Rs. 1,000/-. or with both.

Employee's Compensation Act, 1923:

The formerly known _Workmen's Compensation Act, 1923,' is now known as

_Employee's Compensation Act, 1923, and is an important enactment as it introduced a kind of social security scheme for the workers of this country. It enables an employee in the case of injury and his dependents in the case of his death, to claim the compensation at the cost of his employer organization for such employment injury/ death.

Penalties for Non-Compliance: Compensation should be paid early — delay beyond 1 month, attract interest @6% p.a. and penalty of up to 50% of the compensation. Certain other offences attract fine up to Rs. 500.

Payment of Gratuity Act, 1972:

An employee expects and deserves, as a matter of right, some reward when he retires after a long meritorious service and the enactment of the Payment of Gratuity Act, 1972, has fulfilled this expectation of an employee.

Penalties for Non-Compliance: Non-payment of gratuity payable under the Act is punishable with imprisonment up to 2 years (minimum 6 months) and/or fine up to Rs. 20,000. Other contraventions/offences attract imprisonment up to 1 year and/or fine up to Rs. 10,000.

Employees Provident Funds & Miscellaneous Provisions Act, 1952:

The Employees Provident Funds and Miscellaneous Provisions Act, 1952, is enacted to provide a kind of social security to the industrial workers and it includes following:

- Employees Provident Fund Scheme, 1952
- Employees, Pension Scheme, 1995
- E.D.L.I. Scheme, 1976

The security, however, differs from the kind of security provided under the Workmen's Compensation Act, 1923, or Employees' State Insurance Act, 1948, The Employees' Provident Funds and Miscellaneous Provisions Act mainly provides for the retirement or old age benefits, such as Provident Fund, Superannuation Pension, Invalidation Pension, Family Pension and Deposit Linked Insurance.

Penalties for Non-Compliance: Any person who contravenes any of the provisions of the Act is liable to be arrested without any warrant being issued in respect of a cognizable offence. Whereas defaults by employer in paying contributions or inspections, administration charges attract imprisonment up to 3 years and fines up to Rs. 5,000. In case if offence is repeated, imprisonment may be extended to 5 years but not less than 2.

Bombay Shops & Establishment Act, 1948:

Legislation to regulate the conditions of work in shops and commercial establishments has been in force in the State of Maharashtra for nearly 57 years. The Act is an improved version of The Shop Act, 1939, and has undergone several improvements since its enactment.

Penalties for Non-Compliance: Contravention of certain provisions of Law, penalties for obstructions to the Inspector, non-compliance leading to the prosecution as provided under the Act.

Employees State Insurance Act, 1948:

The Employees' State Insurance Act, 1948, provides to the workers not only accident benefits but also other benefits such as sickness benefits, maternity benefits and medical benefits. Under the Act, the workers are also required to contribute to a social insurance fund which is to be utilized for conferring benefits to them.

Penalties for Non-Compliance: For Employees' Contribution, Imprisonment for 2 years to maximum 5 years and/ or fine of Rs. 25,000/- For Employers' Contribution Imprisonment for 6 months to maximum 3 years and/or fine of Rs. 10,000/-.

Contract Labour (Regulations & Abolitions) Act, 1970:

The Contractor Labour (Regulations & Abolitions) Act, 1970, was passed to prevent exploitation of contract labour. The policy of the Act is to prohibit the employment of contract labour by regulating the same and wherever this is not possible, to improve the conditions of work of contract labour. Apart from providing for prohibition of employment of contract labour, the Act also provides for health and welfare of the contract labour.

Penalties for Non-Compliance: The contractor, for contravening any provisions, can be prosecuted under the Act and can be levied a fine. Contravention of any provisions of the Act shall be punishable with imprisonment to the extent of 3 months or with fine which may extend to Rs. 1,000/- or with both and in the case of continuing contravention, with an additional fine which may extend to Rs. 100/- per day.

Laws related to Equality and Empowerment of Women:

It is discussed under following sub-sections:

- Sexual Harassment of Employees
- The Equal Renumeration Act, 1976

Sexual Harassment of Employees:

Sexual harassment is a type of discrimination based on sex. When someone is sexually harassed in the workplace, it can undermine their sense of personal dignity. It can prevent them from earning a living, doing their job effectively, or reaching their full potential. Sexual harassment can also poison the environment for everyone else. If left unchecked, sexual harassment in the workplace has the potential to escalate to violent behavior. Employers that do not take steps to prevent sexual harassment can face major costs in decreased productivity, low morale, increased absenteeism and health care costs, and potential legal expenses. Employers can prevent many cases of sexual harassment by having a clear, comprehensive anti-sexual harassment policy in place. In cases of alleged sexual harassment, the policy will alert all parties to their rights, roles and responsibilities. Policies must clearly set out how the sexual harassment will be dealt with promptly and efficiently.

Everyone should know about the anti-sexual harassment policy and the steps in place for resolving complaints. This can be done by:

- giving policies to everyone as soon as they are introduced
- making all employees, *etc.* aware of them by including the policies in orientation material
- training people, including people in positions of responsibility, about the policies, and educating them on human rights issues.

An effective sexual harassment policy can limit harm and reduce liability. It also promotes the equity and diversity goals of organizations and institutions and makes good business sense. Employers should monitor their environments regularly to make sure they are free of sexually harassing behaviors. Taking steps to keep a poison-free environment will help make sure that sexual harassment does not take root, and does not have a chance to grow.

The Equal Remuneration Act, 1976:

- It was enacted to Article 39 of the constitution
- The Act provides for the payment of equal remuneration to men and women employees for the same work or work of a similar nature.
- It also provides prevention of discrimination on sex gender against women in matters of employment.

Employees with Special Needs:

The persons with Disabilities Act, 1995

This Act is for people with disabilities. It recognizes that the disabilities people are to be given opportunities that will enable them to integrate with the mainstream society.

Employee Safety at the Workplace:

The Workmen's Compensation Act, 2000

The Act aims to provide workmen and their dependents relief in case of accidents causing death and disablement in course of their employment. Disablement can be classified into

- Total Disablement
- Partial Disablement

Employees' State Insurance Act, 1948

Applicability:

- All factories excluding seasonal factories employing 10 or more persons and working with electric power.
- All factories excluding seasonal factories employing 20 or more persons and working without electric power.
- Any establishment which the Government may specifically notify as being covered.
- Shop employing 20 or more persons.

Eligibility of Employees:

- Any person employed for wages (up to Rs. 6,500) in or in connection with the work of a factory or establishment end.
- Any person who is directly employed by the employer in a factory or through his agent on work which is ordinarily part of the work of the factory or incidental to purpose of the factory.

Benefits:

1) Free medical treatment is offered to covered employees at hospital and dispensaries run by the ESI Corporation.

2) About $7/12^{th}$ of employees normal wage will be payable to him by ESI during sickness.

3) Maternity benefit for 12 weeks of which not more than 6 weeks should be preceding confinement.

4) Injury during/in course of employment resulting in temporary/ permanent disablement entitles the covered employee to a regular payment to substitute his lost wages.

5) Death during course of employment entitles specified dependents to a regular payment.

6) Onetime payment of Rs. 1,500 to help meet funeral expenses.

Records to Be Kept Ready for ESI Inspection:

- Attendance Register/Muster Roll.
- Salary/Wage Register/Payroll.
- EC (Employee‘s & Employer‘s Contribution) Statement.
- Employees‘ Register U/R 32 (Form 7).
- Accident Register U/R 66.
- Return of Contribution (RC-Form 6).
- Return of Declaration Forms (RDF - Form 3).
- Receipted Copies of Challans.
- Books of Account i.e. Cash/Bank, Expense Register, Sales/Purchase Register, Petty Cash Book, Ledger, Supporting Bills and Vouchers, Delivery Challans (if any).

LEAVE FOR EMPLOYEES:

The Leave allocation in employment caters to specific needs of employees during the tenure of his employment. In this regard, the government of India through its policy has scheduled all its leave in form of its eligibility, accumulation, excess of entitlements, encashment and process.

Leave policy in India:

The Government of India has enacted policies for different situations to employees in both government and private organization's. Each of these leaves meet the specific requirements of the employees and the employer is bound to abide by the laid down rules. For women, special leaves like Maternity Leave is enacted, so as to preserve their jobs and also simultaneously take care of themselves &family. Each of the laws have Eligibility, Accumulation, Leave in Excess of Entitlements, Encashment & Process in the list rules.

Leave Schedule:

- It is necessary that leave/s are scheduled in advance and in a manner that balances both the individual‘s desires and hotel‘s need for appropriate coverage on teams and departments.
- Employees in various departments should schedule leave/s with the approval of their department Manager/ Supervisor.

- All other employees should get approval from their supervisor prior to scheduling a leave.
- If a scheduling conflict between employee needs and hotel needs arises, hotel may consider its needs, the needs of the employees' teams, and other relevant factors such as the time period elapsed since an employee's last leave, the length of the prior leave and the role of the employee requesting a leave.
- It is not a certainty that all the leave requests maybe granted; it is strongly recommended by the hotel's employees to obtain approval for leave plans prior to making travel bookings.
- Out of courtesy to co-workers, to notify your Supervisor immediately of any change in leave plans.

Earned Leave:
Eligibility

- All regular, full- time employees are eligible for Earned Leave.
- Earned Leave is calculated on a month on month basis for the calendar year (January –December)
- If you have joined during the middle of the year, your earned leave will be pro-rated from the date you start employment through December 31 of that calendar year.

Entitlement:

- Every month Earned Leave accrues at 13.33 hours per month (equivalent to 1.66 days per month or 160 hours of vacation per calendar year).
- During the probation period of 3 months, you are not entitled to take Earned Leave You may avail your Earned leaves only after completing your probation period, at which point you will have accrued 40 (13.33 hours X 3) hours or 5 days.
- If you are a Management Trainee, your probation period is 1 year. However, you may avail your Earned leaves after completing 3 months of service with the organization, at which point you will have accrued 40 (13.33 hours X 3) hours or 5 days.
- Earned Leave is exclusive of official and weekly holidays. Hence if an employee takes leave during which time a declared holiday or weekend occurs, then those particular date(s) will not be counted as your Earned

Leave.

- Earned leave can be clubbed with Casual Leave.

Accumulation/ Carry forward:

- You are urged to use your Earned Leave time in the year it has accrued.
- However, if you are unable to use all of your accrued Earned Leave during a calendar year, you may elect to carry forward any accrued but unused vacation time into the next calendar year, subject to the maximum accrual level of 240 hours (30 working days).

Hence you can accumulate/ carry forward your earned leaves up to a maximum of 30 days only.

Leave in Excess of Entitlements: This is normally not permitted. However, should there be a need, the employee must apply for the same with full details of the need / reason and the same will be decided on a case to case basis and may be treated as leave with or without pay, purely at the discretion of the Management. This shall require specific approval from the concerned Departmental Heads and HR. The Company may, notwithstanding reason advanced by employee, refuse leave in excess of entitlement in its absolute discretion.

Encashment: Accumulated leaves can be encased during the time of separation. The formula used for calculation of Cashable Leaves is:

Cashable Amount = Monthly Gross (excluding retainers)/ 22* Cashable Leave

Adjustment against notice period

Balance earned leaves cannot be adjusted against the notice period during termination of services.

Process:

To avail earned leave, the employee is required to get his/ her manager's approval.

- Earned leave must be recorded accurately as ―Vacation‖.
- Current earned leave balance and utilized leave will be reflected in the pays lip on a month on month basis

Casual Leave:

Eligibility

- All regular, full- time employees are eligible for Casual Leave.
- Casual Leave is calculated annually for the calendar year (January-December)
- If you have joined during the middle of the year, your casual leave will be pro- rated from the date you start employment through December 31 of that calendar year.

Entitlement:

- Casual Leave shall be credited to the employees account at the beginning of the calendar year. New employees are eligible to use Casual Leave immediately up on hire.
- Casual leave cannot be clubbed more than 3 at a time.
- Casual Leave can be clubbed with Earned Leave.

Accumulation:

- There is no accumulation or carry forward of Casual Leave.

Encashment:

- Casual leave cannot be encased or adjusted against notice pay at the time of separation.

Process:

- An employee can request for Casual Leave to attend to personal matters. These would be granted at the discretion of the Supervisor.
- The employee is required to apply for Casual Leave in advance, unless in case of emergencies where he/she shall submit the leave approval request to the Supervisor within48 hours of resuming duty.
- Casual leave must be recorded accurately in the time sheet as —Time off with pay.

Sick Leave (Medical Leave):
Eligibility

- All regular, full- time employees at Hotels are eligible for Sick Leave

- Sick Leave is calculated annually for the calendar year (January-December)

Entitlement

- An employee is entitled to 7 days of Sick Leave which shall be credited to the employees account at the beginning of the calendar year. New employees are eligible to use Sick Leave immediately upon hire.
- If you have joined in the middle of the year, your Sick leave entitlement will not be pro-rated. The entire Sick Leave of 7 days is granted upon hire.
- Sick Leave cannot be clubbed with Earned Leave or Casual Leave.
- Sick leave is inclusive of weekly holidays.

Accumulation

- There is no accumulation or carry forward of Sick Leave.

Encashment

- Sick leave cannot be encased or adjusted against notice pay at the time of separation.

Process

- Sick leave is to be taken in cases of injury / illness to the employee. An employee must intimate his/ her manager either over the phone or on returning from leave.
- 2 or more days of Sick Leave will require a medical certificate from a qualified and registered medical practitioner. Notwithstanding such certificate, the company can in its sole discretion ask the employee to present himself / herself before the company

Maternity Leave (ML):
The Maternity Benefit Act, 1961

- The Act was passed to provide uniform maturity benefits for women employees in industries not covered by the Employees State Insurance Act.

- Maternity Leave: A female employee is entitled to maternity leave of 12 weeks (6 weeks prior to delivery & 6 weeks after birth of child). An additional 4 weeks can be granted on full pay in case of illness due to pregnancy, delivery miscarriage or premature birth.

Eligibility

- Maternity leave is a statutory leave. All women employees will be entitled to maternity benefits as per the provisions of the Maternity Benefit Act, 1961 and the prevailing State rules.

- Married and expecting women employees are eligible to avail maternity leave.
- Women employees who have completed a minimum of 80 days of continuous service with the company are eligible for maternity leave.
- If you are on probation, you are entitled to avail maternity leave, provided the above condition is fulfilled.

Entitlement

- Maternity leave is restricted to two live births during the service with the company Women employees who have worked for a minimum period of 80 days in the twelve months prior to the delivery shall be entitled to Maternity Leave of up to
- 12 weeks in case of delivery
- 6 weeks in case of miscarriage, from the date of miscarriage
- Under the Act, women employees are eligible for a maximum period of 12 weeks as Maternity Leave and this leave shall not be extended beyond a period of 1 month, without a certificate from a Qualified Medical Practitioner and approval of the HR Personnel.
- All leave/s beyond the statutory limit of 12 weeks will be charged to Earned Leave.
- Maternity Leave may be clubbed with Sick Leave.

Process

- The employee should give at least one month's notice prior to the date of commencement of leave.

- Maternity leave must be recorded accurately in the Oracle time sheet as —Leave of Absence‖
- If you are proceeding on leave beyond the stipulated time, you need to get special approval.

Family and Medical Leave (FMLA):

The Family and Medical Leave Act (FMLA) is a federal law that grants an eligible employee up to 12 weeks of unpaid, job-protected leave in a calendar year when any of the following circumstances are present:

- Birth of a child and/or to care for a newborn child;
- Placement with the employee of a child for adoption or foster care;
- Employee's own serious health condition;
- Care for the employee's spouse, child, or parent with a serious health condition;
- FMLA leave is also granted to care for a domestic partner with a serious health condition under policy and certain collective bargaining agreements.

Eligibility: To be eligible for FMLA benefits, an employee must have:

- At least 12 months of Organisation's service (need not be continuous), and
- At least 1,250 hours of work in the 12 months immediately preceding the leave.

Benefits: The Benefits Office will make the determination of whether an employee qualifies for FMLA leave. Whether an employee's leave is designated as FMLA is not a decision that the employee or supervisor can make independent of the Benefits office. Therefore, it is critical that all supervisors immediately report any medical leave to the Benefits Office to make this determination.

Health Benefits during the Leaves: Under FMLA, an employee may go on intermittent leave taken in separate blocks of time. In addition to 12 weeks of unpaid leave, an eligible employee is entitled to continuation of health benefits during the leave period and restoration to the same or equivalent job if the employee returns within the period allowed under the FMLA. Although FMLA leave is unpaid, Organization's policies and collective bargaining agreements may require or allow an employee to use accrued sick and vacation leave before the employee may go out on leave without pay.

An employee's rights under FMLA can run concurrently with other types of leave. For example, an employee may be eligible for both Workers' Compensation and FMLA benefits because a work-incurred injury could also be a serious health condition that qualifies under FMLA.

ADDITIONAL PROTECTION FOR EMPLOYEES:

Provisions favoring the employment of disadvantaged groups in society, determining the conditions for the use of temporary or fixed-term contracts, or mandated pre-notification periods and severance payments, special requirements for collective dismissals and short- time work schemes influence firing decisions.

Prohibition for Employers: —Serious Health Condition || Defined:

The most common serious health conditions that qualify for FMLA leave are:

- conditions requiring an overnight stay in a hospital or other medical care facility;
- conditions that incapacitate you or your family member (for example, unable to work or attend school) for more than three consecutive days and have ongoing medical treatment (either multiple appointments with a health care provider, or a single appointment and follow-up care such as prescription medication);
- chronic conditions that cause occasional periods when you or your family member are incapacitated and require treatment by a health care provider at least twice a year; and
- pregnancy (including prenatal medical appointments, incapacity due to morning sickness, and medically required bed rest).

Transfer or Reassignment:

If an employee needs intermittent leave or leave on a reduced leave schedule that is foreseeable based on planned medical treatment for the employee, a family member, or a covered service member, including during a period of recovery from one's own serious health condition, a serious health condition of a spouse, parent, son, or daughter, or a serious injury or illness of a covered service member, or if the employer agrees to permit intermittent or reduced schedule leave for the birth of a child or for placement of a child for adoption or foster care, the employer may require the employee to transfer temporarily, during the period that the intermittent or reduced leave schedule is required, to an available alternative position for which the employee is qualified and which better accommodates recurring periods of leave than does the employee's regular position.

Compliance:

Transfer to an alternative position may require compliance with any applicable collective bargaining agreement, federal law (such as the Americans with Disabilities Act), and State law. Transfer to an alternative position may include altering an existing job to better accommodate the employee's need for intermittent or reduced schedule leave.

Occupational Diseases:

Definition: - It is a disease resulting from the exposure during employment to conditions or substances that are determinable to Health. Example: -Black Lung Disease contracted by Miners & Cancer, Tumors by workers in Nuclear Atomic Fuel Plants.

- A Worker contracting an occupational disease is deemed to have suffered an accident out of and in the course of employment.
- The employer is liable to pay compensation to the occupational diseased employees.
- Compensation for Occupational diseases is as per the Categorisation of A, B and C under this Act.

CONSUMER LAWS:

The Consumer Laws are discussed under following sub-sections:

- Definitions - Consumer
- Consumer Protection Act, 1986
- Consumer Grievance Redressal Mechanism in India

Definitions – Consumer:

According to Prof. P. G. Krishanan, consumer means, —***One who pays money or price or cost of goods and deserves to get what he pays for in real quantity and true quality.*** || According to Mr. S. S. Alur, —***A consumer is thus an individual who uses goods and services and purchases goods and services for his final consumption and not for resale or manufacture.*** ||

Consumer Protection Act, 1986:

"DEFECT IN GOODS" means any fault, imperfection or shortcoming in the quality, quantity, potency, purity or standard which is required to be maintained by or under any law for the time being in force under any contract, express or implied or as is claimed by the trader in any manner whatsoever in relation to any goods;

"DEFICIENCY IN SERVICE" means any fault, imperfection, shortcoming or inade- quacy in the quality, nature and manner of performance which is required to be maintained by or under any law for the time being in force or has been undertaken to be performed by a person in pursuance of a contract or otherwise in relation to any service;

Consumer Grievance Redressal Mechanism in India:

The Consumer Grievance Redressal Mechanism Consists of a Three-Tier Structure to deal with the arbitration process, which are explained as follows:

- **District Forum:** It is a dispute redressal body under the purview of State Government, which is constituted at least one in each district or in certain cases one District Forum may cover multiple districts.

- **State Commission:** It is the second tier of dispute redressal mechanism body, constituted by State Government for redressal of the Consumer Grievances at State Level

- **National Commission:** It is the third tier of dispute redressal body, constituted by the Central Government for redressal of the Consumer Grievances at National Level.

District Forum:

Structure: A District Forum Constitutes of a person who is, or has been, or is qualified to be a District Judge, its President and two other members shall be persons of ability, integrity and standing and have adequate knowledge or experience or have shown capacity, in dealing with problems relating to economics, law, commerce, accountancy, industry, public affairs or administration, one of whom shall be a woman.

Scope of Function: The District Forum shall have jurisdiction to entertain complaints where the value of services and compensation claimed **does not exceed Rs. Twenty Lacs.**

A complaint may be filed with a District Forum by:

- A consumer, availing of such service or is agreed to be provided such service;
- Any such recognized consumer association, where the consumer to whom such service is extended or is agreed to be provided with, is a member of such association;
- One or more such consumers, having the interest of similar nature, with the permission of the district forum, on behalf of or for the benefit of all consumers so interested;
- The Central or the State Government.

Complaint/Grievance Redressal Procedure: On receipt of a complaint to the Forum, The District Forum shall:

- forward a copy of such complaint to the opponent, directing him to give his reply/version of the case within a period of 30 days or such extended period not exceeding 15 days as may be granted by the District Forum;

- Where the accused/opponent, on receipt of a copy of the complaint, denies/ disputes the allegations contained in the complaint, or fails to take any action to represent his case within the stipulated time frame given by the District Forum, the District Forum shall proceed to settle the consumer dispute on the basis of the following:

- Evidence/s brought to the notice of the court by the complainant and the opponent, where the opponent denies/ disputes the allegations contained in the complaint.

- Evidence/s brought to the notice of the court by the complainant, where the opponent fails to take any action to represent his case within the stipulated time frame given by the Forum;

- In case of the complainant / authorized representative failing to appear before the District Forum on such day, the District Forum, at its sole discretion, can either dismiss the complaint in default or if a substantial portion of the evidence of the complainant has already been produced/ recorded during the proceedings, decide it on merit basis. The District Forum may decide the complaint ex-parties, in case of the opponent failing to appear for the hearing of the case.

- Notwithstanding the findings, Where any party to a complaint to whom time has been granted fails to produce the evidence / to cause the attendance of his witnesses/ to perform any other such acts, deemed to be necessary for the further progress of the complaint, for which time has been allowed, the District Forum may proceed to decide the complaint forthwith subject to appearance of both the parties. In case of both/any of the parties being absent, the Forum can proceed to decide the case as explained above.

The District Forum may adjourn the proceedings/hearing of the complaint, which shall not exceed more than one such adjournment and the complaint should be decided within 90 days from the date of notice received by the opponent, where complaint does not require any analysis/ investigation and within 150 days if it requires analysis/investigation.

Decision Process/Findings: Based on the proceedings made in the case, If the District Forum is satisfied that any of the allegations contained in the complaint about the services are correct, it shall issue an order to the opposite party directing him to return to the complainant the fee/charges paid, or pay any such amount as may be awarded by it as compensation to the consumer for any loss or injury suffered by the consumer due to the negligence of the opposite party/or, remove the deficiency in the services inquisition / To provide for adequate costs to parties.

Appeal Process: Any Consumer, who is not satisfied with/aggrieved by an order made by the District Forum, may appeal against such order to the higher forum (State Commission) within a period of 30 days from the date of the order. However, in case of delay, the State Commission may entertain such appeal even after 30 days if it is satisfied, that there has been sufficient reason for delay in filing of the appeal.

State Commission:

Structure: The structure of a State Commission consists of a person who is/ has been a Judge of a High Court, who shall be its President; along with two other members.

Scope of Function: The State Commission has jurisdiction to entertain those Complaints where the value of services and compensation **exceeds Rs. 20 Lacs, but not exceeding Rs. 1 Crore** ; and or appeal against the orders of any District Forum within the state/revision petitions against the District Forum.

Complaint/Grievance Redressal Procedure & Decision Process: The State Commission follows the same complaint redressal procedure, similar on the lines of a District Forum.

Appeal Process: Any Consumer, who is not satisfied with / aggrieved by an order made by the State Commission, may appeal against such order to the higher forum (National Commission) within a period of 30 days from the date of the order. However, in case of delay, The National Commission may entertain an appeal even after 30 days if it is satisfied that there has been sufficient reason for delay in filing the appeal.

National Commission:

Structure: The structure of a National Commission consists of a person who is/ has been a Judge of a Supreme Court, who shall be its President (No appointment under this clause shall be made except consultation with the Chief Justice of India); along with four other members having qualifications similar to that of District Forum /State Commission.

Scope of Function: The National Commission has jurisdiction to entertain those Complaints where the value of services and compensation **amount exceeds Rs. 1 Crore** and or appeal against the orders of any State commission/revision petitions against the State Commission.

Complaint/Grievance Redressal Procedure & Decision Process: The National Commission follows the same complaint redressal procedure, similar on the lines of a State Commission. However, the same shall be presented by the complainant/authorized representative to the Commission with the detailed particulars of both the parties, along with the facts related to the complaint & the relevant documents is support of the allegations, and the relief asked for by the complainant.

Appeal Process: Any Consumer, who is not satisfied with / aggrieved by an order made by the National Commission, may appeal against such order to the higher forum (Hon'ble Supreme Court Of India) within a period of 30 days from the date of the order. However, in case of delay, The Supreme Court may entertain an appeal even after 30 days if it is satisfied that there has been sufficient reason for delay in filing the appeal.

General Guidelines Towards Filing an Appeal:

All the Consumer Dispute Redressal Bodies (The District Forum, The State Commission & The National Commission) shall not admit a complaint unless it is filed within 2 years from the date of cause of action taking place. However, in such cases, where there have been sufficient grounds for delay in filing the complaint within the specified period, further extension may be granted by the concerned body.

In the case of such a complaint coming to the District Forum/The State Commission /The National Commission, as the case may be, which is found to be of frivolous nature, it shall, for reasons to be recorded in writing, dismiss the complaint and make an order that the complainant shall have to pay to the opponent such cost incurred in the damage, not exceeding Rs. Ten Thousand Only, or as may be specified in the order

In case of a person against whom a complaint is made/the complainant, failing to comply with any order made by the forums (District Forum/State Commission/National Commission), as the case may be, such person or complainant shall be punishable with an imprisonment, where the term shall not be less than one month but can extend to three years, or with fine, not being less than Rs. Two Thousand, but can extend to Rs. Ten Thousand Only or with both.

HOSPITALITY LAWS:

Hospitality laws were created to ensure that restaurants, hotels, motels, and other public accommodations are providing safety measures within their establishments to ensure the well-being of their patrons. People are expecting to eat good foods when they visit a restaurant. When lodging at a hotel or motel, people are expecting a good night's stay free from any type of harm. They should be protected from any type of criminal activity, such as robbery or assault. What protects us from harm are the laws in place to reduce the chances of these things occurring.

There are many different types of hospitality laws, but one thing they all have in common is the protection of the customer's rights and safety. They also protect customers from being misguided, deceived, or duped by any public establishment.

Who is a Guest?:

Definition: -(As per Hotel's Proprietor's Act, 1956 UK). A traveler shall be a guest during the period commencing with the midnight preceding, and ending with the midnight immediately following, a period for which the traveler was a guest at the Hotel and entitled to use the accommodation so engaged'.

Here, the Guests are of two types namely,

- In – House Guests
- Non-Resident Guests

- To qualify as a Resident Guest, a person has to stay in Hotel Room for a minimum 24 hours
- Non- resident guests are visitors who enjoy the facilities located in the public areas such as all Food & Beverage Point of Sale, Spa's & Business Centre's.

- There are two types of visitors to a Hotel –

- Guests who are invitees of In-House guest's
- Vendor's &Suppliers of Goods and service to Hotel attending meeting with the Management Team.

Duties of a Hotelier towards Guests:

The primary duty of Hoteliers is to welcome guests, provide accommodation and Food & Beverage Services as per standards of the Hotel. A Hotelier is duty bound of –

- Provide Accommodation against confirmed Room Reservation
- Provide Safety & Security to guests and their belongings, which involves -
- Maintaining Guest privacy
- Liability for Loss or damage to guest property
- Bailment
- Responsibility for Guest's lost and found items
- Handling unusual complaints
- Establishing & Maintaining service standards

- Warning guests of any unsafe conditions or areas of the hotel
- Hiring employees who are qualified and well trained in hotel operations
- Handling guests with disabilities
- Circumstances under which hoteliers can deny Accommodation to a guest.
- Circumstances under which Hoteliers can evict a guest
- Serve Food & Beverage responsibly.
- Handle fraud committed by guests

Guest Complaints:

Guest complaints are discussed under following sub-sections:

- Definitions - Complaint
- Complaints Handling in Hotel Industry

Definition - Complaint

"COMPLAINT || MEANS any allegation in writing made by a complainant that—

an unfair trade practice or a restrictive trade practice has been adopted by any trader **or service provider**;

- the goods bought by him or agreed to be bought by him; suffer from one or more defects;
- the services hired or availed of or agreed to be hired or availed of by him suffer from deficiency in any respect;
- a trader or service provider, as the case may be, has charged for the goods or for the service mentioned in the complaint a price in excess of the price –
- *fixed by or under any law for the time being in force*
- *displayed on the goods or any package containing such goods;*
- *displayed on the price list exhibited by him by or under any law for the time being in force;*
- *agreed between the parties;*
- goods which will be hazardous to life and safety when used or being offered for sale to the public, --
- *in contravention of any standards relating to safety of such goods as required to be complied with, by or under any law for the time being in force;*
- *if the trader could have known with due diligence that the goods so offered are unsafe to the public;*
- services which are hazardous or likely to be hazardous to life and safety of the public when used, are being offered by the service provider which such person could have known with due diligence to be injurious to life and safety;||;

<u>Complaints Handling in Hotel Industry</u>

Guest Complaints: When guests are not satisfied with some services and express their discontent to the employees then their grievances are recorded as guest complaints.

Types of Complaints

- Mechanical – Related to non-functioning of equipment's in the room
- Attitudinal – Related to staff.
- Service Related – Related to services provided
- Unusual - Complaints over which hotel has no control

Handling Complaints

- Listen
- Isolate the guest
- Stay calm
- Preserve guest's self-esteem
- Give undivided attention
- Take notes
- Tell guest what can be done
- Set a timeline for action
- Monitor progress
- Follow up

Follow-Up Procedures

- The front office log book is used to
- initiate corrective action,
- verify the guest complaints have been resolved and
- identify recurring problems.
- After the guest has departed, a letter from the front office manager expressing regret about the incident in order to
- Promote goodwill and
- Demonstrate concern for guest satisfaction.
- Then, the front office manager is to telephone the departed guest to get a more complete description of the incident.
- Chain hotels may also receive guest complaints about the hotels in the chain may be compiled and sent to each manager.

Hotel Operation Laws:

- Hotels room rent is payable in advance in order to confirm the bookings.

- Personal food and beverages are strictly not permitted in most of the hotels.

- In India Hotels provide Conference equipment is provided as per actual costs, on prior notice.

- In case any damage is done to the hotel property by guests during their stay, it will be the sole accountability of the guest that made the booking.

Damage to Property: - Guest will be held responsible for any loss and damage to hotel property caused by themselves, their friends or any person for whom they are responsible.

- Extra Bed facility is also offering by the hotels for Adult and Children but only for reasonable price

- Bed tea, Breakfast and evening tea are offers by the hotels but have extra charges for it.

- There are special charges for weekends, Christmas, and New year listed by the Indian Hotels.

- Hotels also charges for Luxury Tax on Room tariff, VAT on Food & Beverages, and corresponding Service Tax applicable as per State-wise Government Regulations.

Credit Card Laws:
Credit Card law in India

- Hotel should check the credit limits from the guest.
- Date of Expiry.
- Card should be from banks approved by RBI.
- Card no. should not appear in the hot bulletin of the bank.
- Amount payable should not cross the credit limit of the hotel or bank.
- The signature of the card holder must tally with credit card signature.
- If the credit limit crosses then authorization should be taken from the bank.

- Authorization number should be mentioned on the credit card charge slip with date.

The name of the hotel and a/c no in bank of hotel must be clear. A credit card is a card issued by bank or financial institution and accepted by a merchant in payment for a transaction for which the cardholder must later pay back the issuer.

<u>**Features of Credit Card in Hotel Operations:**</u>

Foreign Transaction Fees: This is a hidden fee that credit card holders pay, for the most part, unknowingly. If they have not read the fine print of their credit card agreement, most believe that when they purchase something in a foreign currency, the credit card will charge them in dollars after a currency exchange process.

Tighter frequent flier and membership points rules: Once-generous —points programs‖ will become less generous. In some cases, these once-free programs will only come with an annual fee.

Higher priced luxury card programs: Diners Club offers excellent airport club perks for international travelers. Citi has great medical benefits for business travelers who use their cards. Extended warranty benefits double protections offered by manufacturers.

These will all eventually cost more and cardholders in many cases will need to stay alert and sign up to receive the benefits.

Consent for credit limit increases on credit cards: Federally regulated financial institutions have to get your consent before they can increase your credit card limit. If you give verbal consent, the institution must provide confirmation in writing no later than your next statement.

Credit card statements: Federally regulated financial institutions have to include the following information in your credit card statements:

- Time to repay your balance: the credit card issuer must show you an estimate of how long it will take to pay off the current balance in full if you pay only the minimum required every month.
- Advance notice of a fixed interest rate increase: if you have a fixed interest rate credit card and the rate could increase in the next period, the credit card issuer must tell you on your statement the circumstances of the increase and the new rate beforehand.

<u>**Hotels Rules in India During Guest Check-In:**</u>

Mostly the hotels Check-in time is 2 PM and Check-out time is 12 noon.

Management Rights: - The management reserves to itself the absolute right of admission to any person in the hotel premises and to request any guest to vacate his or her room at any moment without any previous notice and without assigning any reason.

As per the Government of India's security regulations, it is mandatory for all guests to show an identity proof (passport for foreigners) at the time of check-in. Please do ensure that you carry this with you.

Proof of Identity: - All guests Foreigners as well as Indian Nationals are required to provide the hotel with valid photographic proof of identity and address proof like Passport, Driving license or Aadhar Card. One must remember pan card is not acceptable as your identity card, also carry the original one.

Guest's Valuables, Cash, Jeweler Etc.: - Visitors are particularly requested to register all the valuables with the hotel management, in case you failed to do so hotel will not be responsible for the loss of guest's belongings.

Hotel Keys: - Hotel keys must be deposited at the reception desk while leaving the hotel, one more thing. This is not permitted to lock the room with personal locks. In case the key is lost and damaged a charge/fine is taken by the hotel management from guests.

Noise and Shouting: - No hotel tolerates the guest who is drunk, rude and absurd behavior, do not shout and watch TV in high volume which may disturb someone else staying in the hotel.

Hazardous Goods: - Storing of hazardous goods like gas cylinders, flammable items, cooking stoves are strictly prohibited.

PUBLIC HEALTH:

The issue of Public health is discussed under following sub-sections:

- Building Code
- Water Supplies, Sewage System and Drainage
- Contagious Diseases
- Guest Elevators and Swimming Pools

Building Code:

A building code, or building control, is a set of rules that specify the minimum acceptable level of safety for constructed objects such as buildings and non-building structures. The main purpose of building codes is to protect public health, safety and general welfare as they relate to the construction and occupancy of buildings and structures. The building code becomes law of a particular jurisdiction when formally enacted by the appropriate governmental or private authority.

In India, each municipality and urban development authority has its own building code, which is mandatory for all construction within their jurisdiction. All these local building codes are variants of a National Building Code, which serves as model code proving guidelines for regulating building construction activity.

Building codes generally include:

Standards for structure, placement, size, usage, wall assemblies, way out of the building rules, size/location of rooms, foundations, floor assemblies, roof structures/assemblies, energy efficiency, stairs and halls, mechanical, electrical, plumbing, site drainage & storage, appliance, lighting, fixtures standards, occupancy rules, even swimming pool regulations. Sounds like a lot but there are nearly infinite ways to build it in a hazardous fashion; contamination, explosion, fire.

- Rules regarding parking and traffic impact
- Fire code rules to minimize the risk of a fire and to ensure safe evacuation in the event of such an emergency
- Requirements for earthquake, hurricane, tornado, flood, and tsunami resistance, especially in disaster prone areas or for very large buildings where a failure would be disastrous
- Requirements for specific building uses (for example, storage of flammable substances, or housing a large number of people)
- Energy provisions and consumption
- Specifications on components
- Allowable installation methodologies
- Minimum and maximum room and exit sizes and location
- Qualification of individuals or corporations doing the work
- For high structures, anti-collision markers for the benefit of aircraft

Water Supplies, Sewage System and Drainage:

Sanitation is the hygienic means of promoting health through prevention of human contact with the hazards of wastes as well as the treatment and proper disposal of sewage wastewater. Hazards can be either physical, microbiological, biological or chemical agents of disease. Wastes that can cause health problems include human and animal wastes, solid wastes, domestic wastewater (sewage, sullage, greywater), industrial wastes and agricultural wastes. Hygienic means of prevention can be by using engineering solutions (e.g. sewerage and wastewater treatment), simple technologies (e.g. latrines, septic tanks), or even by personal hygiene practices (e.g. simple hand washing with soap).

The World Health Organization states that: "Sanitation generally refers to the provision of facilities and services for the safe disposal of human urine and feces. Inadequate sanitation is a major cause of disease world-wide and improving sanitation is known to have a significant beneficial impact on health both in households and across ***communities***‖. The word 'sanitation' also refers to the maintenance of hygienic conditions, through services such as garbage collection and wastewater disposal.

The term "sanitation" is applied to a wide range of subjects such as:

- Improved sanitation - refers to the management of human waste at the household level.
- On-site sanitation - the collection and treatment of waste is done where it is deposited. Examples are the use of pit septic tanks.
- Food sanitation - refers to the hygienic measures for ensuring food safety.
- Environmental sanitation - the control of environmental factors that form links in disease transmission. Subsets of this category are solid waste management, water and wastewater treatment, industrial waste treatment and noise and pollution control.
- Ecological sanitation - an approach that tries to emulate nature through the recycling of nutrients and water from human and animal wastes in a hygienically safe manner.

A clean water supply, especially so with regard to sewage, is the single most important determinant of public health. Destruction of water supply and/or sewage disposal infrastructure after major catastrophes (earthquakes, floods, war, etc.) poses the immediate threat of severe epidemics of waterborne diseases, several of which can be life-threatening.

Water supply systems get water from a variety of locations, including groundwater (aquifers), surface water (lakes and rivers), conservation and the sea through desalination. The water is then, in most cases, purified, disinfected through chlorination and sometimes fluoridated. Treated water then either flows by gravity or is pumped to reservoirs, which can be elevated such as water towers or on the ground (for indicators related to the efficiency of drinking water distribution). Once water is used, wastewater is typically discharged in a sewer system and treated in a sewage treatment plant before being discharged into a river, lake or the sea or reused for landscaping, irrigation or industrial use.

Contagious Diseases:

A **contagious disease** is a subset category of infectious diseases (or communicable diseases), which are easily transmitted by physical contact (hence the name-origin) with the person suffering the disease, or by their secretions or objects touched by them.

Human excreta (waste matter discharged from the body, especially faces and urine) have been implicated in the transmission of many infectious diseases including cholera, typhoid, infectious hepatitis, polio, common cold, measles, chickenpox, cryptosporidiosis, and ascariasis (infection of the intestine with ascarids (parasitic nematode worms). Poor sanitation gives many infections the ideal opportunity to spread: plenty of waste and excreta for the flies to breed on, and unsafe water to drink, wash with or swim in.

Contamination is explained in **food hazards** as harmful substances which is not supposed to be in food. But in this topic, we'll talk about **cross-contamination.**

Cross Contamination:

Some Contamination like *Cross Contamination*, occurs before we receive the food we order. Cross Contamination means transferring of substances to a food from another food or another surface, such as equipment, server's hands. I listed some situations in which cross-contamination occurs.

- Mixing contaminated leftovers with freshly cooked batch of food.
- Handling ready-to-eat foods with unclean hands.
- Handling several kinds of food without washing hands in between.
- Cutting raw chicken, and then using the same cutting board, un sanitized, to cut vegetables.
- Placing ready-to-eat foods on a lower refrigerator shelf and allowing juices from raw fish or meat to drip onto them from an upper shelf.
- Wiping work table with soiled cloth.

For food workers, good **Personal Hygiene** is very important. Because we have bacteria in our body all over our skin, nose, mouth or hands. If these bacteria grow in foods, people who will receive the food will get ill.

Some personal hygiene tips before working in the kitchen:

- Do not work with food if you have any communicable disease or infection.
- Bathe or shower daily.
- Wear clean uniforms or aprons.
- Keep hair neat and clean. Always wear hat or hairnet.
- Keep mustaches and beards trimmed and clean.
- Wash hands and exposed parts of arms before work and as often as necessary during work, including:
- After eating, drinking or smoking
- After use of toilet
- After touching or handling anything that may be contaminated with bacteria
- Cover coughs and sneezes, then wash hands.
- Keep your hands away from you face, eyes, hair and arms.

Guest Elevators and Swimming Pools Lifts:

Passenger lifts and equipment or food lifts must be inspected regularly by a competent person, under the requirements of The Lifting Operations and Lifting Equipment Regulations 1998.

The law requires that all lifts when in use should be thoroughly examined: -

- After substantial and significant changes are made.
- After every 6 months if the lift is used at any time to carry people and every 12 months if it only carries loads, or in accordance with an examination scheme; and
- Following 'exceptional circumstances' such as damage to, or failure of, the lift, long periods out of use or a major change in operating conditions which are likely to affect the integrity of the equipment.

Swimming Pool and Spa Safety:

- You should be considering the following points: -
- Safe storage of chemicals (COSHH).
- Adequate training of staff.
- Adequate supervision of the pool by lifeguards.
- Adequate water disinfection.
- Regular daily testing of the water and recording such tests.

- Adequate signage for warnings.
- All facilities should be protected against unauthorized entry or use.

ENVIRONMENTAL LAWS:

The environmental laws are discussed under following sub-sections:

- Energy Conservation
- Noise Reduction
- Air Quality
- Environmental Global Certification

Energy Conservation:

Energy Conservation Act, 2001

- This Act regulates to save energy by reducing unnecessary energy consumption with purchase of equipment‘s that has a high energy star rating awarded by the Bureau of Energy Efficiency (BEE)
- The Ministry of power, India has implemented the BEE Energy Star Rating systems for electrical appliances since year 2010. The ratings are from one star to five stars. Higher, the star ratings, more is the electrical efficiency of the electrical appliance.

Noise Reduction:

Noise Pollution Rules, 2002

It lays down the terms & conditions that are necessary to reduce noise pollution.

The objective of Noise reduction programs is to contain the levels of noise generated to permitted levels inside the building as well as outside the Hotel building from travelling inside.

Air Quality:

The Air (Prevention& Control of Pollution)Act, 1981

The National Ambient Air Quality Standards (NAAQS) sets the Air Quality Standards in line with developed countries in order to protect public health, vegetation and property.

The Air quality in hotels can be controlled by mixing fresh outside air with the air being circulated inside hotel building after it has been scrubbed to remove impurities.

This involves isolation of air from back -of-the -house areas of the Hotel Example: -Kitchen,Launder, Stores Etc.

Environmental Global Certification:

The Earth Check is an International body that assesses and certifies Hotel Projects on the Agenda 21 Principles for sustainable development endorsed by United Nations Rio Earth Summit 1992.Example: - Novotel Hotel, Hyderabad.

LEEDs Building Certification: LEED Platinum, Gold, Silver Certification: The US Green Building Council (USGBC), awards LEEDs Certification to buildings. LEED stands for Leadership in Energy & Environmental Design. It is the most widely recognized form of Green building certification in the country.

Example: ITC Maurya, New Delhi – LEEDs Platinum Certification, ITC Gardenia, Bangalore – LEEDs Platinum Certification

International organization of standardization (ISO) – ISO 14001 Environmental Standard Certificate: It uses systematic approach to ensure all activities that have an impact on the environment are critically reviewed. **Example:** The Leela Palace Kempinski, Bengaluru; The Taj Gateway, Madurai.

SUMMARY:

The working conditions of employees means - Fixation of working hours, Regular and timely payment of wages, Paid leave & Creation of healthy working environment through basic necessities. **The authorities appointed under the labour act are Inspector,** Labour Commissioner, Additional Labour Commissioner (IR and E), Regional Joint Labour Commissioners, Joint Labour Commissioner (P), Chief Inspector of Plantations, Deputy Labour Commissioner (HQ), Dist. Labour Officer (HQ), Additional Labour Commissioner, Dist. Labour Officers (E), Inspector of plantations & Asst. Labour Officers – Grade II

The major tasks under the are **Trade Union Act, 1926 and the Trade Unions (Amendments)Act, 2001** are to monitor Industrial Relations at the Central Level, Intervention, Mediation and conciliation of Industrial disputes, Intervention in situations of threatened strikes and Lock-outs & Implementation of settlement and Awards. The Laws that Provide for Rights of Employees at Workplace are Employment Exchanges Act , 1959 , The Apprentices Act , 1961 , Shops & Establishment Act , 1948 , The Minimum wages Act , 1948 , The Payment of Wages Act , 2005 , Equal Renumeration Act , 1976 , The Payment of Bonus Act , 1965 , Employees Provident Fund

Scheme(EPF) , 1952 , The Public Provident Act , 1968 , Weekly Holidays Act , 1942 , The Maternity Benefit Act , 1961 , The Worker's Compensation Act , 2000.

Records To Be Kept Ready For ESI Inspection are Attendance Register/ Muster Roll , Salary/Wage Register/Payroll , EC (Employee's & Employer's Contribution) Statement , Employees' Register U/R 32 (Form 7) , Accident Register U/R 66. , Return of Contribution (RC-Form 6) , Return of Declaration Forms (RDF - Form 3) , Receipted Copies of Challans , Books of Account i.e. Cash/Bank, Expense Register, Sales/Purchase Register, Petty Cash Book, Ledger, Supporting Bills and Vouchers, Delivery Challans (if any). **Family and Medical Leave (FMLA) is** a federal law that grants an eligible employee up to 12 weeks of unpaid, job-protected leave in a calendar year when Birth of a child and/or to care for a newborn child , Placement with the employee of a child for adoption or foster care , Employee's own serious health condition , Care for the employee's spouse, child, or parent with a serious health condition , FMLA leave is also granted to care for a domestic partner with a serious health condition under policy and certain collective bargaining agreements. The Directorate General of Resettlement &Employment formulated the Employment Exchange Act. The Equal Renumeration Act, 1976 was enacted to Article 39 of the constitution. The Act provides for the payment of equal renumeration to men and women employees for the same work or work of a similar nature.

The Maternity Benefit Act, 1961 was passed to provide uniform maturity benefits for women employees in industries not covered by the Employees State Insurance Act. Maternity Leave: A female employee is entitled to maternity leave of 12 weeks (6 weeks prior to delivery & 6 weeks after birth of child). An additional 4 weeks can be granted on full pay in case of illness due to pregnancy, delivery miscarriage or premature birth. The persons with Disabilities Act, 1995 is for people with disabilities. It recognizes that the disabilities people are to be given opportunities that will enable them to integrate with the mainstream society. The Workmen's Compensation Act, 2000 aims to provide workmen and their dependents relief in case of accidents causing death and disablement in course of their employment. Disablement can be classified into Total Disablement & Partial Disablement

Occupational Disease: - A Worker contracting an occupational disease is deemed to have suffered an accident out of and in the course of employment. The employer is liable to pay compensation to the occupational diseased employees. Compensation for Occupational diseases is as per the Categorizations of A, B and C under this Act. Energy Conservation Act, 2001 regulates to save energy by reducing unnecessary energy consumption with purchase of equipment's that has a high energy star rating awarded by the Bureau of Energy Efficiency (BEE). The Ministry of power, India has implemented the BEE Energy Star Rating systems for electrical appliances since year 2010. The ratings are from one star to five stars. Higher, the star ratings, more is the electrical efficiency of the electrical appliance. Noise Pollution Rules, 2002 lays down the terms & conditions that are necessary to reduce noise pollution. The objective of Noise reduction programs is to contain the levels of noise generated to permitted levels inside the building as well as outside the Hotel building from travelling inside.

The National Ambient Air Quality Standards (NAAQS) sets the Air Quality Standards in line with developed countries in order to protect public health, vegetation and property The Air quality in hotels can be controlled by mixing fresh outside air with the air being circulated inside hotel building after it has been scrubbed to remove impurities.

GLOSSARY:

Prohibition of unfair labour practice: No employer or workman or a trade union, whether registered under the Trade4 Unions Act, 1926 or not, shall commit any unfair labour practice.

Housing Facilities: - Besides providing semi-furnished house, some hotel companies provide facilities in form of House Rent Allowance (HRA). The HRA will be in proportion of the employee's salary.

Employer means any person who employs one or more employees in any schedule of employment.

Wages means all remuneration capable of being expressed in terms of money.

Employee means any person employed for hire or reward and includes an out – worker.

TRADE Union (definition): - A Trade Union is a voluntary organization of workers pertaining to a particular industry that is formed to balance and improve the relations between employers and employees in form of protection, welfare schemes, interest and collective action of workers.

Occupational Diseases (Definition): - It is a disease resulting from the exposure during employment to conditions or substances that are determinable to Health. Example: -Black Lung Disease contracted by Miners &Cancer, Tumors by workers in Nuclear Atomic Fuel Plants.

Guest (Definition As per Hotel's Proprietors Act, 1956 UK)_A traveler shall be a guest during the period commencing with the midnight preceding, and ending with the midnight immediately following, a period for which the traveler was a guest at the Hotel and entitled to use the accommodation so engaged _

DEFINITIONS – CONSUMER -According to Prof. P. G. Krishanan, consumer means, —**One who pays money or price or cost of goods and deserves to get what he pays for in real quantity and true quality.** ||

DEFECT IN GOODS: means any fault, imperfection or shortcoming in the quality, quantity, potency, purity or standard which is required to be maintained by or under any law for the time being in force under any contract, express or implied or as is claimed by the trader in any manner whatsoever in relation to any goods;

DEFICIENCY IN SERVICE means any fault, imperfection, shortcoming or inadequacy in the quality, nature and manner of performance which is required to be maintained by or under any law for the time being in force or has been undertaken to be performed by a person in pursuance of a contract or otherwise in relation to any service;

UNFAIR TRADE PRACTICE means a trade practice which, for the purpose of promoting the sale, use or supply of any goods or for the provision of any service, adopts any unfair method or unfair or deceptive practice.

RESTRICTIVE TRADE PRACTICE means a trade practice which tends to bring about manipulation of price or conditions of delivery or to affect flow of supplies in the market relating to goods or services in such a manner as to impose on the consumers' unjustified costs or restrictions

Sanitation (Definition by The World Health Organization) - "Sanitation generally refers to the provision of facilities and services for the safe disposal of human urine and feces. Inadequate sanitation is a major cause of disease world-wide and improving sanitation is known to have a significant beneficial impact on health both in households and across communities. _

Earth Check: Green Globe Certification - The Earth Check is an International body that assesses and certifies Hotel Projects on the Agenda 21 Principles for sustainable development endorsed by United Nations Rio Earth Summit 1992.Example: - Novotel Hotel, Hyderabad.

LEEDs Building Certification: LEED Platinum, Gold, Silver Certification: The US Green Building Council (USGBC), awards LEEDs Certification to buildings. LEED stands for Leadership in Energy &

Environmental Design. It is the most widely recognized form of Green building certification in the country.

International organization of standardization (ISO) – ISO 14001 Environmental Standard Certificate: It uses systematic approach to ensure all activities that have an impact on the environment are critically reviewed.

A **contagious disease** is a subset category of infectious diseases (or communicable diseases), which are easily transmitted by physical contact (hence the name-origin) with the person suffering the disease, or by their secretions or objects touched by them.

FOUR

FOOD AND BEVERAGE LAWS OF INDIA

INTRODUCTION:

The Government of India. constituted a Central Advisory Board of Health in1937 and the Food Adulteration Committee in 1943. These two bodies recommended a Central Act which was passed after the Independence. The Prevention of Food Adulteration Act, 1954 incorporated many of the suggestions made by the Central Advisory Board of Health.

IMPORTANT LEGAL TERMS:

Food'(Definition): Food means any substance, whether processed, partially processed or unprocessed, which is intended for human consumption and includes primary food, genetically modified or engineered food or food containing such ingredients, infant food, packaged drinking water, alcoholic drink, chewing gum, and any substance, including water used into the food during its manufacture, preparation or treatment but does not include any animal feed, live animals unless they are prepared or processed for placing on the market for human consumption, plants prior to harvesting.

Primary Food (As per Food Safety and Standards Act, 2006): —Primary Food‖ means an article of Food, being a product of agriculture or horticulture or animal husbandry and dairying or aquaculture in its natural form, resulting from the growing, raising, cultivation, picking, harvesting, collection or catching in the hands of a person other than a farmer or fisherman. _

Adulterant (As per the Prevention of Food Adulteration Act, 1954):

—Adulterant—means any material which is or could be employed for the purpose of adulteration.'

Food Additives (As per Food Safety and Standards Act,2006): _Food Additive _ as any substance not normally consumed as food by itself or used as a typical ingredient of the food , whether or not it has nutritive value , the intentional addition of which to food for a technological purpose in the manufacture , processing , preparation , treatment , packing , packaging , transport or holding of such food results , or maybe reasonably expected to result , in it or its by-products becoming a component of or otherwise effecting the characteristics of such food but does not include 'Containments' or substances added to food for maintaining or improving nutritional qualities.

FOOD LEGISLATION AND FOOD SAFETY AND STANDARD'S ACT:

Food legislation and food safety and standard's act is discussed under following sub- sections:

- Food Safety and Standard's (FSS) Act
- The Food Safety and Standards Authority of India (FSSAI)
- The Food Safety and Standards Act, 2006

Food Safety and Standard's (FSS) Act:

- Multiplicity of food laws, standard setting and enforcement agencies for different sectors of food
- Varied Quality/Safety standards restricting innovation in food products.
- Thin spread of manpower, poor laboratories infrastructure and other resources non-conducive to effective fixation of standards
- Standards rigid and non-responsive to scientific advancements and modernization.
- Poor Information dissemination to consumer level

Important points in The Food Safety and Standards (FSS) Act:

- Compels the establishment of food practices only which are permitted.
- Compulsory licensing and registration of food business.
- Only registration necessary for – Petty Food Beverage Operators (FBO).
- Compulsory to follow Food Safety System e.g. HACCP/FSMS
- To ensure food safety and quality.

- To increase the shelf life of food products.
- To ensure and keep a check that standard permitted chemicals and additives are only used to protect health of the consumers.
- Prohibits advertisements which are misleading or deceiving or contravenes the provisions of the Act (stakeholders at source may be prosecuted).
- All imports of articles of food are covered.
- Self-Regulation by FBOs to ensure that the articles of food satisfy the requirements of this Act at all stages of production, processing, import, distribution and sale within the businesses under his control.
- Provision for graded penalties where offenses like manufacturing, storing or selling misbranded or sub-standard food is punished with a fine, and more serious offences with imprisonment or both.

The Food Safety and Standards Authority of India (FSSAI):

The Food Safety and Standards Authority of India (FSSAI) is a Statutory Regulatory Body under Ministry of Health & Family Welfare, Government of India as a Single Point of Reference for All Matters Relating to Food Safety and Standards in India. FSSAI has been created for laying down science-based standards for articles of food and to regulate their manufacture, storage, distribution, sale and import to ensure availability of safe and wholesome food for human consumption.

The Food Safety and Standards Authority of India (FSSAI) constitutes representation form representative of Food Industry, Food Technologists, Producers, Retailers, Consumers, Farmers, State Governments and concerned ministries. Compulsory of laying down science-based standards for articles of food and to regulate their manufacture, storage, distribution, sale and import to ensure availability of safe and wholesome food for human consumption.

The Food Safety and Standards Act, 2006:

Passed by parliament with the intention to cover 08 different food laws in to one comprehensive Act. The Various Acts & orders were replacing to make one act the FSS Act are:

- Solvent Extracted Oil, De-oiled Meal & Edible Flour (Control) Order 1967
- Fruit Product order 1955
- Meat Food Products Order 1973
- Food Safety & Standards Act 2006

- Edible Oils Packing 1998
- Vegetable Oil Products Order1988
- Milk & Milk Product Amendment Regulations- Prevention of Food Adulteration Act 1954

A FOOD SAFETY MANAGEMENT SYSTEM (FSMS):

A food safety management system (FSMS) is discussed in following sub-sections:

- A Food Safety Management System (FSMS)
- Good Practices
- Food Additives

A Food Safety Management System (FSMS):

It is a network of interrelated elements that combine to ensure that food does not cause adverse human health effects. These elements include programs, plans, policies, procedures, practices, processes, goals, objectives, methods, controls, roles, responsibilities, relationships, documents, records, and resources. The Purpose of FSMS is to ensure the manufacture, storage, distribution and sale of safe food.

Key Elements A Food Safety Management System (FSMS):

The five basic key elements of Food Safety Management System (FSMS) are:

- Good Practices/ PRPs (Pre-Requisite Programs- basic guidelines for food safety)
- Hazard Analysis /HACCP
- Management Element / System
- Statutory and regulatory requirements
- Communication

Good Practices:

Good Practices/ PRPs (Pre-Requisite Programs- basic guidelines for food safety): For this reason, Senior Management need to understand the benefits of an effective Food Safety Management System:

- A Food Safety Management System structured with the principles of HACCP will have a clear focus on food safety which is a fundamental requirement of any food business

- An effectively implemented and applied HACCP based Food Safety Management System will improve customer confidence in the safety of food
- A Food Safety Management System based on HACCP takes a preventative approach that is designed to reduce liabilities.
- An effective Food Safety Management System demonstrates management commitment to the supply of safe products.
- Food Safety Management System Records provide evidence of due diligence (carefulness)
- HACCP based Food Safety Management Systems can be combined with other management systems such as ISO 9001:2008. This combination provides a Food Safety based system also considers quality
- Certification to the International Standard ISO 22000 gives all interested parties a clear message that the organisation is serious about Food Safety

Good Manufacturing Practices (GMP): It is good, systemic, scientific practice for the benefit of the manufacturer &customer. To apply the GMP in particular area we have to be aware of the particular followings:

Food Additives:

Food additives be defined as any substances or a mixture of substances, other than basic food stuff, which is present in food as a result of any aspect of production, processing, storage or packaging.

In other way food additives are the substances which are added to food by the manufacturers to facilitate processing or to improve appearance, texture flavor &keeping quality. It added to food for maintaining or improving nutritional qualities.

HAZARDS:

There are various factor affecting **Food Safety**, the biggest one being **Food Hazard.** Food hazard can be defined as a biological, chemical or physical agent in a food, or condition of a food, with the potential to cause an adverse health effect.

Different Type of Hazards:

- **Physical Hazard** – Any foreign materiel not normally found in food, which may cause illness by using the products. Example - glass, hair, stones, plastic, bone, jute, matchstick, feathers etc.

- **Biological Hazards** – Microorganism that causes diseases are termed asfood borne pathogens. There are three type of food borne diseases- infection, intoxication, and toxicities. Example – Microbiological pathogenic bacteria, Spore forming, non-spore forming – parasites, protozoa, virus.

- **Chemical Hazards**- Any chemical contaminants introduced in food system which may causes illness to the individual using the products. Examples- colours, flavours, pesticides, adulterants, cleaning chemicals, Veterinary residues etc.

Related Terminologies:

Risk assessment

Risk assessment is defined for the purposes of the Codex Alimentarius Commission as "A scientifically based process consisting of the following steps:

a. Hazard identification,
b. Hazard characterization,
c. Exposure assessment,
d. Risk characterization.

Hazard identification is "The identification of biological, chemical, and physical agents capable of causing adverse health effects and which may be present in a particular food or group of foods."

Hazard characterization is "The qualitative and/or quantitative evaluation of the nature of the adverse health effects associated with biological, chemical and physical agents which may be present in food. For chemical agents, a dose-response assessment should be performed. For biological or physical agents, a dose-response assessment should be performed if the data are obtainable."

Exposure assessment is "The qualitative and/or quantitative evaluation of the likely intake of biological, chemical, and physical agents via food as well as exposures from other sources if relevant."

Risk characterization is "The qualitative and/or quantitative estimation, including attendant uncertainties, of the probability of occurrence and severity of known or potential adverse health effects in a given population based on hazard identification, hazard characterization and exposure assessment." Hazard identification, hazard characterization, exposure assessment will help to know the adverse health effect.

The Hazard Analysis and Critical Control Points (HACCP):

The Hazard Analysis and Critical Control Points (HACCP)is an international principle defining the requirements for effective control of food safety. HACCP **compliance** helps organizations focus on the hazards that affect food safety and hygiene, and systematically identify them by setting up control limits at critical points during the food production process.

The Hazard Analysis and Critical Control Points (HACCP):

Certification: It enables you to demonstrate your commitment to food safety and customer satisfaction, as well as continuously meeting the expectations of a changing world.

The Hazard Analysis and Critical Control Points (HACCP):

Requirements: It includes the implementation of the seven principles plus five other preliminary steps.

Preliminary Steps of The Hazard Analysis and Critical Control

- Points (HACCP)
- Assembly of the HACCP team
- Describe product
- Identify the intended use
- Construct Flow diagrams
- On-site confirmation of flow diagrams

The Seven Principles of The Hazard Analysis and Critical Control Points (HACCP):

Principle 1: Conduct a hazard analysis. - Plans determine the food safety hazards and identify the preventive measures the plan can apply to control these hazards. A food safety hazard is any biological, chemical, or physical property that may cause a food to be unsafe for human consumption.

Principle 2: Identify Critical Control Point (CCP). - A Critical Control Point (CCP) is a point, step, or procedure in a food manufacturing process at which control can be applied and, as a result, a food safety hazard can be prevented, eliminated, or reduced to an acceptable level.

Principle 3: Establish critical limits for each critical control point. - A critical limit is the maximum or minimum value to which a physical, biological, or chemical hazard must be controlled at a critical control point to prevent, eliminate, or reduce to an acceptable level.

Principle 4: Establish critical control point monitoring requirements. - Monitoring activities are necessary to ensure that the process is under control at each critical control point.

Principle 5: Establish corrective actions. - These are actions to be taken when monitoring indicates a deviation from an established critical limit. The final rule requires a plant's HACCP plan to identify the corrective actions to be taken if a critical limit is not met.

Principle 6: Establish record keeping procedures. - The HACCP regulation requires that all plants maintain certain documents, including its hazard analysis and written HACCP plan, and records documenting the monitoring of critical control points, critical limits, verification activities, and the handling of processing deviations.

Principle 7: Establish procedures for ensuring the HACCP system is working as intended. - Validation ensures that the plants do what they were designed to do, that is, they are successful in ensuring the production of a safe product.

Benefits of The Hazard Analysis and Critical Control Points(HACCP):

- It is a systemic approach covering all aspects of food safety, from raw material growth, harvesting and purchase to the final product.
- Use of HACCP will move a company from an end product testing approach towards a preventive quality assurance.
- HACCP provides cost effective control of food borne diseases
- Use of HACCP leads to reduced product loss.
- Use of HACCP focuses technical resources into critical part of the process.
- HACCP complies legal requirement.

If you are required to have your management systems certified against a multiple international safety or quality standard, you can combine the parallel requirements with HACCP and cover them cost effectively with a single food audit.

Responsibility and Authority:

It is discussed under following sub-sections:

- Management Element / System
- Local Level

- Food Safety Site Level

Management Element / System:

The Managing Director: Will ensure that there is an effective policy for food safety within operational areas, and take a direct interest in the food safety programme.

- Will support all persons carrying out their responsibilities under this policy.
- Will ensure adequate resources are available to meet food safety requirements.
- Will ensure that responsibilities are properly assigned, entered into job descriptions and accepted at all levels.

Other Executive Directors: Will support the Managing Director in ensuring that there is an effective policy for food safety within operational areas, and take a direct interest in the food safety programme.

- Will support all persons carrying out their responsibilities under this policy.
- Will ensure adequate resources are available to meet food safety requirements.
- Will ensure that responsibilities are properly assigned, entered into job descriptions and accepted at all levels.

Quality Assurance Manager: Responsible for all food safety and hygiene for Allied Foods ensuring at all sites staff are adhering to food hygiene legislation and following the HACCP plan for the site/contract and will ensure that the site managers provide sufficient resources, in terms of personnel & equipment, are employed in order to achieve the required performance levels.

Local Level:

Contract Manager / General Manager / Site Managers: Responsible for all food safety and hygiene for site/contract ensuring all staff are adhering to food hygiene legislation and following the HACCP plan for site/contract. The CM/GM will ensure that sufficient resources in terms of personnel & equipment are employed in order to achieve the required performance levels.

First Line Managers / Team Leaders: Responsible for the supervision of staff with regard to food hygiene in your area, ensuring all staff are adhering to food hygiene legislation and following the HACCP plan for the site.

Food Safety Site Level:

Each site will be responsible for appointing a Food Safety coordinator who will have responsibility and authority:

- To manage a food safety team and organise its work
- To ensure relevant training and education of the food safety team members
- To ensure that the company food safety management system is implemented, maintained and updated
- To report to the Quality Assurance Manager on the effectiveness and suitability of the food safety management system.

The Hazard Analysis and Critical Control Points (HACCP) Team: Each site/contract **shall** establish and train a HACCP Team. This team should be multidisciplinary meet regularly and conduct regular audits. Audit records are an integral part of this requirement, and documentation of specific assignments and actual accomplishments **shall** be maintained. Follow-up audits should be done to ensure that items are corrected. Regularly monitor documentation that may indicate trends of non-conformance and recommend corrective actions

General Responsibilities of Employees: Responsible for adhering to food hygiene relevant to your role and adhering to the site/contract HACCP plan.

- All staff must take ownership of the food safety and hygiene systems in operation. All Employees:
- Are responsible for adhering to food hygiene relevant to your role and adhering to the HACCP plan for the site.
- Adhere to food safety instructions

- Operate hygienically
- Report any problems relating to food safety or a failure in control measures
- Comply with the law.
- Work in accordance with any training or instruction given.

- Follow any food safety arrangements and rules established for the protection of the food chain.
- Make use of any food safety or protective equipment or devices supplied.
- Food handlers are expected to report illnesses that may impact on food safety.

COMMUNICATION:

It is discussed under following sub-sections:

- External Communication
- Internal Communication

External Communication:

It is important that we ensure sufficient information on issues concerning food safety is available throughout the food chain and, in order to do this, we have identified a number of key relationships that we intend to maintain:

Suppliers and Contractors: All our suppliers will complete questionnaire and undergo a vetting and monitoring processes that ensures they have effective food safety arrangements in place. All contractors are briefed on food safety requirements before work commences.

Customers: Allied will, in collaboration with its customer, continuously examine the latest industry techniques, technology and equipment with a view to improving food safety performance. Such improvements may be required as a result of new or changing legislation. If Allied takes on additional work or contracts work out the process or company will be audited to ensure the food safety procedures are safe.

Statutory and regulatory authorities: We have a procedure to record and communicate within the business all aspects of working with statutory and regulatory authorities. All commitments and plans agreed are documented and communicated to the central health and safety team in the monthly board report.

Professional bodies: We work closely with consultancies, training providers and many other advisory bodies to ensure that we keep abreast of changing legislation and best practices in the area of food safety.

Internal Communication:

It is company policy to establish a HACCP team for all food sites The objectives of the HACCP team meetings are:

- Food Safety Representative
- Contract/General Manager
- As required, representatives from Warehouse, Stock and Admin and Transport management.
- As required, representatives from the shop floor.

FOOD SAFETY AND STANDARDS:

It is discussed under following sub-sections:

- Prevention of Food Adulteration Act, 1954 (PFA)
- Authorities under Prevention of Food Adulteration Act (PFA)

Prevention of Food Adulteration Act, 1954 (PFA):

The Prevention of Food Adulteration Act, 1954 (PFA) broadly lays down the principles of Food Laws regarding prevention of Food Adulteration. According to PFA act an article of food shall be deemed to be adulterated:

- If the article sold by a vendor is not of the nature, substance or quality demanded by purchaser and is to his prejudice, or is not of the nature, substance of quality which it purports or is represented to be
- If the article contains any other substance which affects, or if the article is so processed as to affect injuriously the nature, substance or quality thereof
- If any inferior or cheaper substance has been substituted wholly or in part for the article so as to affect injuriously the nature as substance or quality thereof.
- If any constituent of the article has been wholly or in part abstracted so as to affect injuriously the nature, substance or quality thereof
- If the article had been prepared, packed or kept under unsanitary conditions whereby it has become contaminated or injurious to health
- If the article consists wholly or in part of any filthy, putrid disgusting, rotten, decomposed, or diseased animal or vegetable substance or is insect- infested or otherwise unfit for human consumption
- If the article is obtained from a diseased animal
- If the article contains any poisonous or any ingredient which renders its contents injurious to health
- If the container of the article is composed, whether wholly or in part of any poisonous or deleterious substance which renders its contents

injurious to health.

- If any coloring matter other than that prescribed in respect thereof and in amounts not within the prescribed limits of variability is present in the article
- If the article contains any prohibited preservative or permitted preservative in excess of the prescribed limits
- If the quality or purity of the article falls below the prescribed standards or its constituents are present in quantities which are in excess of the prescribed limits of variability.

Authorities under Prevention of Food Adulteration Act (PFA):
Food Inspector:

- The State Commissioner of Food Safety, shall, by notification, appoint such persons as it thinks fit, having the prescribed qualifications as Food Inspectors for such areas as it may assign to them for the purpose of performing its functions under this Act.
- The State Government may authorize any officer of the State Government having the prescribed qualifications to perform the functions of a Food Inspector within the specified jurisdiction.

Powers of Food Inspector:

- To take sample of any food article from
- Any person selling such article
- Any person who is in the course of delivering or preparing to deliver such article to a purchaser or consignee. A consignee after delivering of any such article to him.
- To send such sample for analysis to the public analyst (PA) of local area. When the food inspector wants to lift suspected food the shop keeper must first be told. There should be a witness present when the food inspector lifts the sample.

Public Analyst: The Central or State Government my, by the notification of the official gazette, may appoint such persons as it thinks fit, having the prescribed qualifications to be public analyst for such local areas as may be assigned to them:

Provided that no person who has any financial interest in the manufacture, import or sale of any article or food shall be appointed to be a pubic analyst under this section:

Provided further that different public analysts may be appointed for different articles of food.

Report of Public Analyst:

- The public analyst shall deliver a report in the prescribed form to Local (Health)
- On the receipt of report, if analysis report suggests that the food is adulterated, the Local (Health) Authority shall prosecute the concerned persons within ten days from the date of receipt of the copy of the report.
- The certificate issued by **the Director of Central Food Laboratory** shall supersede the report given by the public analyst in case of any discrepancy.
- Any document purporting to be report signed by a public analyst can be used as an evidence of facts in the court of law unless superseded by the Director of Central Food Laboratory.

Powers of Court: Notwithstanding anything contained in the **Code of Criminal Procedure, 1973 (2 if 1974),** all offences shall be tried summary way by a **Judicial magistrate** of the first calls especially empowered in this behalf by the State Government or by a Metropolitan Magistrate and the provisions of sections 262 to 265 of said code shall, as far as may by, apply to such trail:

- Provided that in case of any conviction in a summary trail under this section, it shall be lawful for the magistrate to pass a sentence of imprisonment for a term not exceeding one year:
- Provided further that when at the commencement of, or in the course of, a summary trail under this section it appears to the magistrate that the nature of the case is such that a sentence of imprisonment for a term exceeding one year may have to be passed or that it is, for any other reason, undesirable to try the case summarily, the magistrate shall after hearing the parties, record an order to that effect and thereafter recall any witness who may have been examined and proceed to hear of rehear the case in the manner provided by the said Code.

FOOD SAFETY MANAGEMENT SYSTEM (FSMS) PROGRAM:

It is discussed under following sub-sections:

- Structure of the Food Safety Management System (FSMS) Program
- Preparation of the documents for Food Safety Management System (FSMS) Program
- Reference Documents for Food Safety Management System (FSMS) Program
- Document and validation of Food Safety Management System (FSMS) Program
- Conclusion

Structure of the Food Safety Management System (FSMS):

Program: FSMS Program will cover following documents

- The FSMS Plan (samples are provided as guidance) and
- Flow chart of for the Process
- A self-inspection checklist, which is to be submitted as an annexure to the plan.

FSMS guideline document is attached which has detailed the checklist/ flowchart and FSMS plan for various categories. The categories which are not covered can use general checklist which is given in guideline document. These documents will need to be submitted by the FBO as part of application for new license or renewal of license. Also, the FSSAI approved audit agency may inspect the FBOs on basis of this scope.

Preparation of the documents for Food Safety Management System (FSMS) Program:

- Use guideline documents for preparation of the FSMS program. The guideline document is to be used only for reference purpose - to understand how to make the flow chart and FSMS plan.
- Schedule 4 checklists are given category-wise that should be used for self-checking purpose.
- The categories which are not covered can use general checklist.
- For compliance of Schedule 4 & FSMS Plan, the reference documents are attached with the program to facilitate the FBOs in development of individual FSMS Program.

Reference Documents for Food Safety Management System (FSMS) Program:

In order to support the implementation and give clarity to FBOs, the FSMS implementation reference document has been provided which can be used. These documents are for guidance; and some changes may be required depending on type of food business. These documents have covered following

- Implementing Schedule IV Requirements – Guidance.
- Conducting a Food Safety Assessment and Developing a FSMS Plan – Guidance.

Document and validation of Food Safety Management System (FSMS) Program:

The Mandatory documents shall be validated by respective Food Safety Officer/Designated officer or he may assign suitable agency/person who is competent to carry out this job.

Record

- Food Safety Management System (FSMS) Plan Form
- Self-Inspection checklist (Schedule IV)
- Flow chart

Conclusion: The Food Safety Management System is a continual process and every FBO should aim for improvement and take higher Food Safety objectives for consumer safety.

FACILITY AND EQUIPMENT CLEANING, SANITATION AND PEST CONTROL PROCESS:

The facility and equipment cleaning, sanitation and pest control process is discussed in following sub-sections:

- Establishment grounds and facilities
- Standards for equipment cleaning

Establishment grounds and facilities:

- grounds and pest control
- construction

- lighting
- ventilation
- plumbing
- sewage disposal
- water supply and water, ice, and solution reuse
- dressing rooms/lavatories
- Equipment and utensils
- Sanitary operations
- Employee hygiene
- Tagging insanitary equipment, utensils, rooms, or compartments

Standards for equipment cleaning:

- Equipment and utensils must be of such material and construction to facilitate cleaning and be maintained in a sanitary condition.
- Equipment and utensils must not be constructed, located, or operated in ways that prevent their inspection.
- Containers used to store inedible products must not create insanitary conditions.
- Inspect equipment brought into the facility to ensure that it can be cleaned and inspected properly
- Ensure that equipment is maintained properly (i.e., no flaking belt material on conveyors, no loose parts that can fall into product, or no loose parts that are constructed of material that may adulterate product)
- All food and non-food contact surfaces must be cleaned and sanitized as frequently as necessary.
- Cleaning compounds, sanitizing agents, and processing aids must be safe and effective under the conditions of use.
- Product must be protected from adulteration during processing, handling, storage, loading, and unloading.

LIQUOR LICENSING:

Liquor is a liquid intoxicant, deriving its intoxicating potency from the ethyl alcohol in it. Liquor can be divided into three broad categories, namely Indian Made Foreign Liquor (IMFL), Beer and Country Liquor. Hard liquors broadly have alcohol content of and above 20% and denote Whisky, Rum, Brandy, the white spirits like Gin and Vodka and also include Country Liquor. Soft liquors have a range of 4-20% of alcohol and include Beer,

Cedar, Wines (Fermented Alcoholic Beverages) and Liquor's.

In Indian markets most prominent segment of liquor consumed by the middle classes, is the Indian Made Foreign Liquor, which covers most liquor, barring beer and country liquor, and is available in glass or sometimes plastic bottles. Beer is also available in glasses filled through dedicated taps dispensing what is known as draught beer. Most Indian beer is Lager that is it can be stored for some time. and all of them use an herb, known as hops, for flavoring. Liquors from which sugar content has been chemically reduced are termed as "dry". Country Liquor is generally in the range of 25% of alcohol and also available in glass bottles only. Wines in India are available in red or white variety, with pink almost none existing. Champagne, generally a ceremonial drink, also known as sparkling wine, is generally off-white and is fizzy because of its carbonation at the time of bottling. Liqueurs are concentrated syrups, available in myriad flavors, and are usually taken without dilution after major meals.

Liquor Legislation in India:

- In year 1862, the then British government in Imperial India licensed the first brewery and introduced taxes
- The Punjab Excise Act, 1914 defines the terms like Liquor, Country Liquor and
- Foreign Liquor. It is in the Punjab Excise Liquor Act, 1954; the term Imported Foreign Liquor was enacted.
- After Independence of Republic India, the Indian Government desire was to implement Prohibition in the Country. This objective of the then government has been clearly stated in the Article list of the Directive Principles of State Policy of Indian Constitution.

Alcohol Law in India & Delhi:

Alcohol is a subject in the State List under the Seventh Schedule of the Constitution of India. Therefore, the laws governing alcohol vary from state to state. Liquor in India is generally sold at liquor stores, restaurants, hotels, bars, pubs, clubs and discos. Some states, like Kerala and Tamil Nadu, prohibit private parties from owning liquor stores making the state government the sole retailer of alcohol in those states. In some states, liquor may be sold at groceries, departmental stores, banquet halls and/or farm houses. Some tourist areas have special laws allowing the sale of alcohol on beaches and houseboats. Home delivery of alcoholic beverages is illegal in

Delhi. However, Delhi permits home delivery of beer and wine by private vends and departmental stores. The sale of beer at departmental stores, banquet halls and farm houses, is legal in Delhi.

EXCISE POLICY FOR THE YEAR 2013-14: (For Symbolic understanding) Readers are requested to check the latest Excise policy on their respective State Government's websites.

The said liquor policy is discussed under following sub-sections:

- On Individuals
- For Special Occasions
- Liquor Vends
- Tavern

On Individuals Possession limit: -

Quantity of purchase and possession of liquor by an individual from L-2/ L-14-A for Country liquor\IMFL, Beer and Wine is kept unchanged & fixed as under:

- Country Liquor: - 2 Bottles of 750 ML
- IMFL/IFL: - 18 Bottles of 750 ML
- Beer: - 36 Bottles of 650 ML
- Wine: - 18 Bottles of 750 ML.

Private Possession permit (L-50): -The possession of liquor by L-50 permit 20 Along with fee is fixed as under: -

The fee for the grant of L-50 shall be Rs 500/ for a year and Rs 3000/ for life time. The private possession limit will be as under. (Please check the latest updates)

- IMFL/IFL 36 Quarts of 750 ML
- Beer 72 Bottles of 650 ML
- Wine 36 Bottles of 750 ML

Working Hours: - 10 AM to 11 PM throughout the year.

Excise Duty on Denatured Spirit: -

The Excise Duty on denatured spirit will be **leviable @Re.1.25/- per BL.**

For Special Occasions:

Fee of Permit on Functions/Celebration (L-42): Permit fee @ Rs. 1500/- per day per function is to be charged on the permit allowing service of liquor on special occasions.

Liquor Vends:

Location of Liquor vends: No liquor vend shall be permitted to be opened near (not less than 50-meters from main gate of any) place of worship, educational institution & place of public entertainment. The liquor vend on the National Highway/ State Highway are required to be located strictly as per the provisions stipulated in the Punjab Scheduled Roads & Controlled Area (Restriction of Unregulated Development) Act, 1963. No liquor vend shall be allowed to be opened at a distance of less than 150 meters of National Highway (except within Municipal Corporation) limits. The distance shall be measured from the main entrance of the liquor vend. Administration reserves the right to refuse permission for a particular location for the reasons of public morality, public health and public order

Checking by Health Department: No officer of any other department to take action or check the quality of liquor produced and sold in U.T., Chandigarh except along with the Excise Officer not below the rank of Excise Inspector.

VAT on Country Liquor/IMFL/ Beer/Wine, etc.: VAT on Country Liquor, IMFL, Beer, Wine, etc. is kept unchanged @12.5%. 14.

Tavern:

- Tavern to continue both with Country Liquor (L-14A) and IMFL (L-2) vends at license fee of Rs. 70,000/- and Rs. 1.50 lacs respectively for a 21 period of twelve months commencing from 1st May, 2013 to 30th April, 2014.
- The Tavern shall be located in separate premises from the vend by metes and bounds.
- Tavern attached to L-2 vend to have eight tables (minimum) with seating capacity of 40 persons, to have temperature control system within the premises, clean and modern toilets and cutlery and crockery of good standard. Tavern attached to country liquor vends `to have attached toilets, neat & clean premises and cutlery and crockery of good standard.
- In order to further improve the ambience and functioning of Tavern attached to L-2 vends the following conditions will be mandatory for grant of the license.
- To have provision for metered electric and water supply.

- To have proper system of garbage collection and disposal.
- To have a separate kitchen.
- To have tiled flooring in kitchen, seating hall and toilets.
- To have family enclosures
- To provide meal

The Collector may refuse to grant a license for Tavern in exercise of the powers conferred under section 35 of the Punjab Excise Act, 1914 as applicable to UT, Chandigarh.

Grouping and clubbing of vends: No grouping and clubbing of vends will be allowed.

Strength of liquor to be sold: Standard strength of IMFL to be sold in U.T. Chandigarh shall be 75 degree. Also, Excise Commissioner is empowered to allow sale of IMFL/IFL of any strength other than the standard strength to facilitate opening up market to all reputed/popular brands of low alcohol content.

Checking of vends by Police Officer: Gazette officers of the rank of DSP and above to check the excise vends after taking with him an excise officer not below the rank of Excise Inspector.

Revalidation Fee of Permits: Revalidation fee @ of Re.0.75/- per B.L. is to be charged for the revalidation of the Permits whose validity has expired.

Size of Excise Bottles: The size of bottles to be as given below

1. 750 ML: - All type of liquor except beer.
2. 375 ML: - All type of liquor except beer.
3. 180 ML: - All type of liquor except beer.
4. 90 ML: - All type of liquor except beer.
5. 1000 ML: - IMFL/IFL. 6.
6. 1.25 L: - IFL.
7. 2.25 L: - IFL
8. 4.5 L: - IFL
9. 650 ML: - Beer.
10. 325/330 ML: - Beer.
11. 500 ML: - Beer.
12. 275 ML: - RTD (Ready to drink like Teachers with coke/soda, Bacardi with cola) & Wine.
13. 60 ML: - IMFL/IFL

The Excise & Taxation Commissioner may allow any other size in case of imported liquor and reputed/popular IMFL brands.

- 20. Bottling Plants: - The renewal fee of B.W.H.-2 (Bottling Plant License) is fixed at Rs. 8.5 lacs for a period of twelve months commencing from 1st May, 2013 to 30th April, 2014.
- Further, the bottling plant licensees will be granted D-2 license to redistill the rectified spirit to improve the quality of their products on the payment of license fee of Rs.2.5 lacs for a period of twelve months commencing from 1st May, 2013 to 30th April, 2014.
- In case of new B.W.H.-2 licenses, a fee of Rs.13.00 lacs will be charged for issuing Letter of Intent (LOI) for establishing a B.W.H.-2 license in U.T. The license fee for new B.W.H.-2 license is fixed at Rs.32 lacs and the fee of LOI will be adjustable if the applicant fulfills the conditions of LOI within 6 months of the date of issue of the LOI within the same financial year.
- Further, the license fee of L-11 & L- 15 licenses issued to the B.W.H.-2 licenses is fixed at Rs.1,50,000/- & Rs.40,000/- respectively for a period of twelve months commencing from 1st May, 2013 to 30th April, 2014. 21.
- License fee of Wholesale and Retail sale license of denatured spirit (L-17): - The annual license fee of Wholesale & Retail sale License of Denatured Spirit for a period of twelve months commencing from 1st May, 2013 to 30th April, 2014 is fixed as under: -

    - Wholesale: Rs.22,000/-
    - Retail sale: Rs.4500/-

Introduction of Holograms: - The use of Holograms on packing /bottles of country liquor, Indian Made Foreign Liquor & Imported Foreign Liquor (excluding Beer, Wine, Champaign, Liqueurs and RTD etc.) will be introduced during the Excise year 2013-14 and the cost of Holograms will be borne by the licensee. Further, this provision will not be applicable on liquor sold at L-9 licensee.

Hours of Sale of Alcohol in Hotels in India

- In Bars: 5:00 p.m. – 11: 45p.m., but the hours of sale vary from state to state.
- In Dining Areas: Can be served with meals.

- Dry Days are specific days when the sale of alcohol is banned. National holidays such as Republic Day (January 26), Independence Day (August 15) and Gandhi Jayanti (October 2) are usually dry days throughout India

PROHIBITION:

Prohibition is one of the routes that certain state governments in India have adopted in order to regulate & curb the Socio-economic impact of Alcoholism. Example: - Prohibition in the state of Manipur in form of Manipur Liquor Prohibition Act,1991.

The Bombay Prohibition Act, 1949 regulates the sale, consumption and transportation of Alcohol& makes it mandatory for a person to acquire a drinking permit.

Possession limit for liquor:

Liquor being an excisable article cannot be stored by a person like any general commodity. Possession limit has therefore been prescribed. Any individual person can possess at his residence alcoholic beverages within the prescribed limit for bonafide consumption by him and by members of his family or his guests.

Note: An individual is allowed to carry one unsealed bottle of 750 ml. while entering into the National Capital Territory of Delhi from other States.

Dry Days:

The dry days of **15th August** and **26th January** to be observed up to**05:00 PM** and **2nd October** for whole day. The dry-days as notified/directed by the Election Commission of India/State Election Commission will also be observed as Dry Days.

LIQUOR LICENSING PROCEDURE:

The liquor licensing procedure is discussed under following sub sections:

- Liquor Licenses
- Off Premises License
- On Premises License
- General Restriction on Licenses
- Mandatory Compliance of a Liquor License
- Sale of Alcohol to a Drunken Person & Intoxication

Liquor Licenses:

A liquor license is a permit to sell alcoholic beverages. The issue of Liquor License is either Off Premises License or On Premises License. The applicant has to submit the following documents along with the application on the prescribed format as per the local govt.

Off Premises License:

Grant of L-1 License:

- Every year Government of Delhi formulates the Excise Policy and in pursuance to this policy all the liquor Licenses (L-1) are granted for the wholesale vending to a Company or a society or a partnership firm or proprietorship firm provided the applicant owns distillery / breweries / manufacturing units/bottling plants.
- The applications for the grant of License are invited through the public notice published in some of the leading newspapers.
- An application for the grant of L-1 License is required to be made in response to the public notice in the prescribed format together with its Appendices ('B' and 'C') to the Collector of Excise. The prime job of L-1 Licensee is to supply liquor to the holders of L-2, L-3, L-4, L-5, L-19 and L-19 A, L-52, L-53 licenses in the National Capital Territory of Delhi.
- The aspirants for the grant of L-1 Licenses have to comply with the procedure as laid down in the terms and conditions for the grant of L-1 Licenses which are made available in the Office during the notice period.
- The IMFL/beer brands proposed to be sold by applicant on L-1 License should be owned by the distillery and in respect of IMFL brands excluding wine, the applicant should be in possession of trade mark certificate in respect of these brands.

On Premises License:

L-3/L-5 License in Hotels:

i. L-3 License Fee (Service of Liquor in a hotel to the residents in their rooms)
ii. L-5 License Fee (Service of Liquor in a bar or restaurant attached to a hotel)
iii. Department grants license to hotels (holding star classification and approval of Department of Tourism, Govt. of India).Service of liquor is restricted to specified premises of bar and restaurant only. Hotel is required to submit application on its letterhead accompanied by the

following documents:

- Documentary proof regarding legal status of the hotel i.e. whether it is a company, partnership firm etc.
- Completion certificate of the hotel building.
- Trade license (Local Authority i.e. MCD/NDMC)
- Lodging House license (Local Authority)
- Certificate of registration of eating House license (DCP {Licensing)}
- Documentary proof regarding applicant being an
- Income Tax Assessed and
- Sales Tax-Assessed.
- Layout plan of the hotel, site plan of the license outlets

The Structure of License Fees: The Structure of License Fees payable by Hotels to the Excise department for acquiring an L-3License to serve alcohol in the Rooms and L-5 License to serve Liquor in Restaurants are varied from State to State. You are requested to check the local State Govt website for the License rates.

L-19 License:

Granted for service of liquor/beer in a club:

The applicant is required to apply on the letterhead of the club to the office of the Commissioner of Excise and the accompanying documents are to be as below:

Registration certificate in respect of club

The applicant is required to apply on the letterhead of the club to the office of the Commissioner of Excise and the accompanying documents are to be as below:

- Registration certificate in respect of club.
- Documentary proof in support of legal possession of the plot of the club.
- NOC from the area DCP.
- List of members of the club.
- List of the office bearers of the club.
- Resolution passed by the Management Committee to start the bar facility in the club and also to meet the liability thereof.

L-20 License:

It is granted to licensed hotels, restaurants and clubs for service of foreign liquor inside/outside their licensed premises on temporary basis for hosting a function on a specific day.

Any eligible hotel, restaurant and club can apply for grant of L-20 license after depositing Rs 3000/- as license fee. (Check for Local govt updates please)

General Restriction on Licenses:

Important Information for All Licensees

- You as the licensee are responsible for the activities of employees and patrons in all parts of the licensed premises, even if you are not always physically present, to ensure that the business is operating in accordance with the Law. It is important to strike a balance between the quality of life in the neighborhood and the successful operation of your business.
- Appropriate books and records detailing purchases with invoices and the amount of each sale must be maintained at the premises and made available for inspection.
- Your license certificate must be displayed so that it is in a conspicuous place inside the premises near the point of sale. Copies of the certificate for posting purposes are not acceptable.
- You must have a valid bond in effect at all times.
- Purchases of alcoholic beverages must be made from duly licensed manufacturers and wholesalers. Purchases from retail stores or from any other retail licensee for resale are not permitted.
- Gambling of any type, either professional or social, is not permitted on any licensed premises. Exceptions are the sale of lottery tickets when licensed by the Division of the Lottery and bingo or games of chance when authorized by the State Racing and Wagering Board.
- Refilling or tampering with the contents of any container containing alcoholic beverages is not permitted.
- An alcoholic beverage must be dispensed from the container in which it was received from the wholesaler.
- If you wish to make any changes in the structure of your corporation, or if you wish to change the individuals on the license, you must file the appropriate application and obtain approval from the Authority before making these changes.
- Any plans to make major physical changes or to substantially alter the licensed premises in any way may require permission from the Authority

prior to construction. You are advised to contact your local Zone office to determine if permission is required.

- Please display the warning signs, provided by the Authority when your license was issued, in a conspicuous location in your establishment, as close as possible to the point of sale.

Limitations of Granting License:

- Any person who has been declared insolvent by any court in India, who is insane or who is below 25 years of age.
- Any person who has been convicted by a criminal court for any non-bailable offence.
- Any person who is not assessed to income tax.
- No licensee shall employ any person suffering from an infectious or contagious disease.
- No person shall print or publish in any newspaper / book / leaflet for display or distribute any advertisement or other matter soliciting the use of or offering any liquor.
- L-4 license for service of IMFL/Beer may only be granted to an independent restaurant approved by the Department of Tourism of Govt. of India.
- The business premises of a licensee shall be kept closed on all dry days.
- The hours for the sale of liquor shall be such as may be specified in an order by the Excise Commissioner.
- The licensee shall sell liquor at the price fixed by the Excise Commissioner.
- The licensee shall prominently display in front of his shop a signboard showing the retail price of each brand of liquor to be charged by him.
- No person shall have in his possession any quantity of any intoxicant, knowing the same to have been unlawfully imported, transported, manufactured, cultivated or collected, or knowing the prescribed duty not to have been paid thereon.
- No licensed vendor shall sell or deliver any liquor or intoxicating drug to any person apparently under the age of twenty-five years whether for consumption by such person or by another person and whether for consumption on or off the premises of such vendor.
- No person who is licensed to sell any liquor or intoxicating drug for consumption on his premises shall, during the hours in which such

premises are kept open for business employ or permit to be employed, either with or without remuneration, any man under the age of 25 years or any woman in any part of such premises in which such liquor or intoxicating drug is consumed by the public.

- Consumption and service of liquor at public places is completely banned.
- Consumption of liquor is injurious to health

Mandatory Compliance of a Liquor License:

The Mandatory requirements in order to meet the compliance of Liquor License are as follows: -

- The display of the License in the prominent place of the Restaurant or Bar premises; preferably near the entrance of the point of sale (POS)
- Stock the Bar with Alcoholic Beverages purchased in the Export Capital Goods (EPCG) Scheme or under an Open General License (OGL).
- Record the Inventory in the excise register that is stamped and signed by the Inspector.
- The Inventory of the Alcoholic Beverages is maintained in 'Units'.
- The Liquor store is to be located within the Hotel premises. The Location is to be cleared specified in the Floor Plan, which is submitted to the authorities at the time of placing the Application.
- All purchases are to be made as per the Individual License issued to the Restaurants &Bars.

Sale of Alcohol to a Drunken Person & Intoxication:

Sale of Alcohol to a Person who is Drunk: Section 141 makes it an offence to sell or attempt to sell alcohol to a person who is drunk, or to allow alcohol to be sold to such a person on relevant premises.

Sub-section 2 applies to:

- any person who works at the premises in a capacity, whether paid or unpaid, which gives him the authority to sell the alcohol concerned;
- the holder of a premises license in respect of the premises;
- the designated premises supervisor (if any) under such a license;
- any member or officer of the club which holds a certificate who at the time the sale (or attempted sale) takes place is present on the premises in a capacity which enables him to prevent it; and
- the premises user in relation to the temporary event notice in question.

This section applies in relation to the supply of alcohol by or on behalf of a club to or to the order of a member of the club as it applies in relation to the sale of alcohol.

A person guilty of an offence under this section is liable on summary conviction to a fine not exceeding level 3 on the standard scale.

It is now an offence under the 2003 Act to supply alcohol to a drunken person and to admit a drunken person to a bar. Any license holder that allows this to occur on their premises is liable on summary conviction to a class B fine for a first offence and a class A fine for any subsequent offence.

- Do Not Make A Sale to An Intoxicated Individual
- Recognize the Signs of Intoxication
- Look for:
- bloodshot eyes
- slurred speech
- mood swings
- the smell of alcohol
- loud, abusive, profane language
- staggering or falling

SALE OF CIGARETTES AND TOBACCO:

Sale of the Tobacco products in India is regulated by the following Laws: -

- Cigarette & Other Tobacco Products (Prohibition of Advertisement & Regulation of Trade and Commodities production, supply &distribution)Act, 2003
- Cigarette & Other Tobacco Products (Prohibition of Advertisement & Regulation of Trade and Commodities production, supply &distribution)Act, 2004

Cigarettes and other Tobacco Products Act, 2003:

(Prohibition of Advertisement and Regulation of Trade and Commerce, Production, Supply and Distribution)

About the Act: ***'Smoking in India'*** is prohibited in public since 2 October 2008 under Prohibition of Smoking in Public Places Rules, 2008 and Cigarettes and Other Tobacco Products (Prohibition of Advertisement and Regulation of Trade and Commerce, Production, Supply and Distribution)

Act, 2003. The nationwide smoke-free law pertains only to public places.

Permitted Smoking Zones:

Smoking is allowed on roads, inside one's home or vehicle. Smoking is also permitted in airports, restaurants, bars, pubs, discothèques and some other enclosed workplaces if they provide designated separate smoking areas. Anybody violating this law will be charged with a fine of Rs 200.

Prohibition:

Prohibition of smoking in a public place: Places where smoking is restricted include auditoriums, movie theatres, hospitals, public transport (aircraft, buses, trains, metros, monorails, taxis,) and their related facilities (airports, bus stands/stations, railway stations), restaurants, hotels, bars, pubs, amusement centers, offices (government and private), libraries, courts, post offices, markets, shopping malls, canteens, refreshment rooms, banquet halls, discothèques, coffee houses, educational institutions and parks.

At least one should be at the entrance of the public place and one at noticeable place(s) inside, containing the warning —**No Smoking Area-Smoking here is an offence** —.

Prohibition in the hotel:

- The owner or the manager or in charge of the affair of a hotel having thirty rooms or restaurants having seating capacity of thirty persons or more shall ensure that,
- The smoking and non-smoking areas are physically segregated.
- The smoking area shall be located in such manner that the public is not required to pass through it in order to reach the non-smoking area.
- Each area shall contain boards indicating thereon —**Smoking Area/ Non- Smoking area** ‖ .

Prohibition of advertisement of cigarette and other tobacco products:

- The size of the board used for advertisement for cigarettes and any other tobacco products
- It Should be displayed at the entrance or inside a hotel where cigarettes and any other such tobacco products are offered for distribution or sale
- The display shall not exceed 90 cm by 60 cm and number of such boards shall not exceed two.

- Each such board shall contain in the Indian language as applicable, one of the following warning, namely: - ***Tobacco Causes Cancer,*** or ***Tobacco Kills***
- The board shall contain only the brand name or picture of the tobacco products and no other promotional message and picture

Prohibition of sale to minors: The owner or the manager or the In charge of the hotel or restaurants where cigarettes and other tobacco products are sold shall display a board of minimum size of 60cm by 30cm at noticeable place(s) containing the warning *"Sales of tobacco products to a person under the age of eighteen years is a punishable offence"*, in Indian language(s) applicable.

Applicability of The Cigarettes and other Tobacco Products Act, 2003: The Cigarettes and other Tobacco Products Act, 2003 states that - Restaurants with more than 30 covers & Hotels with more than 30 Rooms can permit smoking in designated areas. These areas are to be segregated & displayed with signage 'Smoking Area'.

SUMMARY:

The Government of India. constituted a Central Advisory Board of Health in1937 and the Food Adulteration Committee in 1943. **FSS Act** is the Multiplicity of food laws, standard setting and enforcement agencies for different sectors of food and Varied Quality/Safety standards restricting innovation in food products. **The Food Safety and Standards Authority of India (FSSAI)** The Food Safety and Standards Authority of India (FSSAI) is a Statutory Regulatory Body under Ministry of Health & Family Welfare, Government of India as a Single Point of Reference for All Matters Relating to Food Safety and Standards in India.

The Seven Principles of The Hazard Analysis and Critical Control Points (HACCP) Principle 1: Conduct a hazard analysis, Principle 2: Identify, Principle 3: Establish critical limits for each critical control point., Principle 4: Establish critical control point monitoring requirements., Principle 5: Establish corrective actions., Principle 6: Establish record keeping procedures., Principle 7: Establish procedures for ensuring the HACCP system.

Prohibition: -Prohibition is one of the routes that certain state governments in India have adopted in order to regulate & curb the Socio-economic impact of Alcoholism. Example:

- Prohibition in the state of Manipur in form of Manipur Liquor Prohibition Act, 1991 **Dry Days:** - The dry days of **15th August** and **26th**

January to be observed up to **05:00 PM** and **2nd October** for whole day. The dry-days as notified/directed by the Election Commission of India/State Election Commission will also be observed as Dry Days.

L-3 License Fee (Service of Liquor in a hotel to the residents in their rooms)

L-5 License Fee (Service of Liquor in a bar or restaurant attached to a hotel)

L-19 License - Granted for service of liquor/beer in a club

The Cigarettes and other Tobacco Products Act, 2003 - The Cigarettes and other Tobacco Products Act, 2003 states that - Restaurants with more than 30 covers & Hotels with more than 30 Rooms can permit smoking in designated areas. These areas are to be segregated & displayed with signage 'Smoking Area'.

GLOSSARY:

'Food' (Definition): Food means any substance, whether processed, partially processed or unprocessed, which is intended for human consumption and includes primary food, genetically modified or engineered food or food containing such ingredients, infant food, packaged drinking water, alcoholic drink, chewing gum, and any substance, including water used into the food during its manufacture, preparation or treatment but does not include any animal feed, live animals unless they are prepared or processed for placing on the market for human consumption, plants prior to harvesting.

Primary Food _(As per Food Safety and Standards Act, 2006): Primary Food‖ means an article of Food, being a produce of agriculture or horticulture or animal husbandry and dairying or aquaculture in its natural form, resulting from the growing, raising, cultivation, picking, harvesting, collection or catching in the hands of a person other than a farmer or fisherman.

Adulterant (As per the Prevention of Food Adulteration Act, 1954): —Adulterant

—means any material which is or could be employed for the purpose of adulteration.

Food Additives (As per Food Safety and Standards Act, 2006): _Food Additive _ as any substance not normally consumed as food by itself or used as a typical ingredient of the food , whether or not it has nutritive value , the intentional addition of which to food for a technological purpose in the manufacture , processing , preparation , treatment , packing , packaging , transport or holding of such food results , or maybe reasonably expected to result , in it or its by-products becoming a component of or otherwise effecting the characteristics of such food but does not include _Containments' or substances added to food for maintaining or improving nutritional qualities.'

Food Additives - Food additives be defined as any substances or a mixture of substances, other than basic food stuff, which is present in food as a result of any aspect of production, processing, storage or packaging.

Hazard identification is "The identification of biological, chemical, and physical agents capable of causing adverse health effects and which may be present in a particular food or group of foods."

Hazard characterization is "The qualitative and/or quantitative evaluation of the nature of the adverse health effects associated with biological, chemical and physical agents which may be present in food. For chemical agents, a dose-response assessment should be performed. For biological or physical agents, a dose-response assessment should be performed if the data are obtainable."

Exposure assessment is "The qualitative and/or quantitative evaluation of the likely intake of biological, chemical, and physical agents via food as well as exposures from other sources if relevant."

Risk characterization is "The qualitative and/or quantitative estimation, including attendant uncertainties, of the probability of occurrence and severity of known or potential adverse health effects in a given population based on hazard identification, hazard characterization and exposure assessment." Hazard identification, hazard characterization, exposure assessment will help to know the adverse health effect.

Physical Hazard – Any foreign materiel not normally found in food, which may cause illness by using the products. Example - glass, hair, stones, plastic, bone, jute, matchstick, feathers etc.

Biological Hazards – Microorganism that causes diseases are termed as food borne pathogens. There are three type of food borne diseases- infection, intoxication, and toxicities. Example – Microbiological pathogenic bacteria, Spore forming, non-spore forming – parasites, protozoa, virus.

Chemical Hazards- Any chemical contaminants introduced in food system which may causes illness to the individual using the products. Examples- colors, flavors, pesticides, adulterants, cleaning chemicals, Veterinary residues etc.

The Author

Dr Anshumali Pandey, PhD, Author.

Dr. Anshumali Pandey, is a renowned & reliable name in the field of Education, Hospitality, Tourism and Tribal Food. He is a Teacher and Chef by profession, and also an Author, a Business Auditor, and an avid culinary traveller to the Indian Sub continental hinterlands. Dr. Anshumali Pandey is a Hospitality Educator (PhD) who specialises in Higher Education, Office Administration, Pay roll, HR, Labour Laws, Audit, and Procurement & Tender Process. He is an Author with 50 Publications consisting of 35 Books.

The books written by Dr Anshumali Pandey are essentially a banquet arising from an experience of over 25 years of Professional life and have boiled down to crisp and accurate writing on his favourite subjects. Hospitality Sector champion requires to be a specialist in many fields and Dr Pandey is one of them. His knowledge is evident from the spectrum of subjects which he has chosen for his books so far, which ranges from being a specialist chef, to Master of Human resources, to Education and to love for children, and topped with Spirituality.

Books written by the Author are –

1. Theory of Indian Cookery

2. Beauty and Irony of Silvassa Tourism
3. A Short Indian Food Story
4. Be Your Own Guide to Indian Cuisine
5. Cookery Fundamentals
6. History of Indian Food
7. The Great Indian Story Book for Children
8. Personal Budget: Easy Work Book
9. Online Classes Log Book
10. Dictionary Making Work Book for School Children
11. The Lazy Bed
12. Hindu Dharm (हिन्दू धर्म) (In Hindi Language)
13. Where is my coffee?
14. Your First Job is Never your Last (Volume 1)
15. You are Almost There (Quick Fix Resume and Interview Hacks)
16. Working for the Enemy? - A lesson in Career Management
17. Public Speaking for the Young
18. A Date With Coffee
19. How to be The Best Hotel Front Office Employee
20. Diploma in Food Production, The complete Syllabus
21. Diploma in F&B Service, The Complete Syllabus
22. Diploma in Front Office, The Complete Syllabus
23. The Time to Speak is Now
24. Munshi Premchand (Short Stories in English)
25. The Housekeeping Department, Text Book
26. Hitchhiker's Guide to Trekking in Uttarakhand
27. Uttarakhand, A divine Land for a Reason
28. Bachhon ke liye rochak kahaniyan (बच्चों के लिए रोचक कहानियाँ) (In Hindi Language)
29. Basic Communication Skills of English
30. The Basic Office Organisation Book for Start-ups
31. Hospitality HRM
32. Hospitality Marketing
33. Bakery Ingredients and Tools
34. Human Resource Management for Indian Professionals
35. The process of LAWFULLY operating a Hospitality business in India

Connect with me: anshumali.pandey@gmail.com

https://notionpress.com/author/337004

Please scan the QR code for complete information about the Author and his Works.

Printed by Libri Plureos GmbH in Hamburg,
Germany